THINK AND ACT ANEW

*How Poverty in America Affects Us All
and What We Can Do about It*

Larry Snyder

Foreword by E. J. Dionne, Jr.

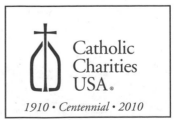

Catholic
Charities
USA®

1910 • Centennial • 2010

ORBIS BOOKS
Maryknoll, New York 10545

Biblical citations are from the Oremus Bible Browser, http://bible.oremus.org/ (accessed June 10, 2010), *The New Revised Standard Version*, Anglicized Edition (The Division of Christian Education of the National Council of the Churches of Christ in the United States of America, 1995).

Library of Congress Cataloging-in-Publication Data

Snyder, Larry, 1941-
 Think and act anew : how poverty in America affects us all and what we can do about it / Larry Snyder.
  p. cm.
 ISBN 978-1-57075-904-8 (pbk.)
 1. Economics—Religious aspects—Catholic Church. 2. Social justice—Religious aspects—Catholic Church. 3. Church and social problems—Catholic Church. 4. Church and social problems—United States. 5. United States—Economic conditions—20th century. 6. United States—Economic conditions—21st century. 7. United States—Social conditions—20th century. 8. United States—Social conditions—21st century. I. Title.
 BX1795.E27S59 2010
 261.8'3250973—dc22
                    2010027997

"When you're growing up you don't realize how poor you are."

(Raul Lozano, 55, the son of farm workers, who formed La Mesa Verde, which helps residents of San Jose's low-income neighborhoods grow their own organic produce.)

"When he was growing up he picked onions and string beans to earn money for school clothes, his boots mended with copper wire. Until 1969, when the family was finally able to buy a home, he lived without hot water or cooking gas."

(Patricia Leigh Brown. "In Latino Gardens, Vegetables, Good Health and Savings Flourish," *San Jose Journal*, January 16, 2010)

Contents

Foreword
Bringing Catholic Social Thought (Back) to Life

E. J. Dionne, Jr.

A Baptist friend who is a divinity school professor tells me that one of her favorite classes every year involves introducing her mostly Protestant students to Catholic social teaching. She sees Catholic social thought as a gift to the entire Christian tradition, a carefully thought-through system of ideas that links charity, justice, social action, and public policy. This proud daughter of the Baptist tradition would not for an instant think of changing churches, but she sees in Catholic social thought a set of rigorously grounded commitments that enrich us all.

A Jewish friend who does not consider himself much of a religious believer came away delighted with Pope Benedict XVI's encyclical *Caritas in Veritate*, seeing it as one of the best moral critiques he had encountered of the underlying causes of the financial crisis. I had not before heard this friend quote a religious document with such passion or enthusiasm.

I bring up my two friends not to engage in a progressive version of Catholic triumphalism, but to suggest something quite different: that rank-and-file Catholics do not appreciate the splendor of what the Catholic Church teaches about how to build a more just society rooted in the common good. It should be something of a scandal for us that our friends and collaborators outside the Church have often spent far more time pondering the implication of Catholic social thought than we Catholics have.

At Georgetown University where I teach, some of my very

7

best Catholic students speak of never having encountered the Church's social tradition in their religious education classes. Of course they know where the Church stands on abortion. But that it has had a great deal to say over the years about economic justice, social welfare, and the God-given dignity of all human beings *after* they are born surprises many of them.

Only rarely do priests celebrating Sunday Mass offer their congregations homilies rooted in what the Church teaches about the right ordering of society—and this despite the heroic efforts of Father Ray Kemp and his "Preaching the Just Word" project aimed at encouraging our clergy to do just that. On the whole, I have found, nuns tend to speak far more about Catholic social thought than do others in the Church, partly because so many of them live the word daily in hospitals, schools, homeless shelters, and wherever else there is service to be performed in bettering lives and saving souls. Yet except in the schools or when they are sick, most rank-and-file Catholics only occasionally encounter the extraordinary work done by the sisters and the message their labor and their words send about the Church's mission.

So much of the work they and other social missionaries carry out would be impossible absent Catholic Charities, another of the Church's genuine gifts to the world. Long before anyone heard the words "faith-based organization" and the now well-known acronym, FBO, Catholic Charities was supporting and performing the corporal and spiritual works of mercy. Not to put too fine a point on it, Catholic Charities USA began its work a century ago, which would put it more than eight decades in advance of our large public argument about the proper role of partnerships between government and church-based charitable groups.

So it's not at all surprising that Father Larry Snyder, the president of Catholic Charities USA, has taken on the task of updating Catholic social thought in light of Pope Benedict's teaching and bringing it back to life for a Church that should be doing much more to carry its social message to the world. Father Snyder is operating within a long-established tradition, but *Think and Act Anew* is resolutely contemporary in its argument. It relentlessly cuts through the rigid categories to which our contemporary debate is enslaved and is stubbornly practical in offering remedies that have promise for the here and now. For many, it will be their first introduction to the power of Pope Benedict's recent encyclical, which challenges the fixed views of just about everyone.

One can hope that Father Snyder's book has the same salutary impact on our time that Father John A. Ryan, the great innovator in American Catholic social thinking, had with his 1906 book, *A Living Wage*. Lew Daly, the author of *God's Economy*, believes that Father Ryan and the subsequent Catholic proposals he inspired (notably the 1919 Bishops' Program of Social Reconstruction) powerfully shaped the New Deal. One would like to think Father Snyder's work will somehow find its way into the hands of our next FDR.

Catholic social thought has always been at its best when it offered its message not simply to Catholics but to society as a whole—to my Baptist and Jewish friends and thousands like them. I can imagine that many non-Catholics (including nonbelievers) who are searching for a morally coherent approach to economic justice in the wake of the financial crisis that bred the Great Recession will find inspiration here.

Yet the Church's social teaching has been most effective when Catholics themselves realized its richness and allowed it to enter—and alter—their way of approaching political and social problems. Liberals and conservatives alike have much to learn from what Father Snyder says, and the many millions who think of themselves as moderates will warm to his refusal to cater to ideological prejudices. There is and long has been a Catholic Third Way that respects the market's role but does not deify any economic system and acknowledges the market's shortcomings. The Catholic Third Way asserts an important role for government in fostering social justice (Catholics are not government-haters, or at least shouldn't be), but it also celebrates the indispensible role played by organizations outside government in building community, strengthening social bonds, and delivering assistance in ways that government cannot.

Father Snyder offers four economic principles that, if taken seriously and put into practice, would revolutionize our approach to the dismal science. His ideas also challenge every talk show host and pundit to abandon simple-minded sloganeering and cheap-shot polemicizing.

First, the market must not be a place where the strong subdue the weak. Economics and finance are not themselves dangerous instruments, but they become so when they are used for purely selfish ends. . . .

Second, we recognize that the market is an effective tool—and can even be a beneficial one for the exchange of goods and services that give us what we need and want. The market economy of the United States has enabled an era of innovation and development unprecedented in the history of mankind. But it is also subject to *distributive justice* and *social justice* because there is a broader social and political context in which it operates, and which it needs to function.

Third, "every economic decision has a moral consequence." In the global economy in which we now live, we cannot rely on a simplistic formula that allows economic activity to be free-wheeling and relies on government structures alone to assure that the wealth created is distributed. In a year that has seen banks fail, mortgages foreclose, and huge corporations that pay no U.S. taxes, it is clear to us that a new way of thinking and acting in our economic sphere is needed.

Finally, in the words of Pope Benedict XVI: *"The economy needs ethics in order to function correctly*—not any ethics whatsoever, but an ethics that is people-centered."

Anyone (again, including non-Catholics) looking for the place to start the debate we need to have in the wake of the financial crisis would do well to begin exactly where Father Snyder does.

But this is not simply a book of principles. It is also a work of passion. For Father Snyder and his colleagues at Catholic Charities see poverty up close, every day. Those who have been excluded from the mainstream of economic life—those suffering for reasons having absolutely nothing to do with their own decisions or actions, and those who have made mistakes for which they are asked to pay too much—are not statistics on a page for the men and women of Catholic Charities. They are not abstractions, stereotypes, or stick-figures. They are living, breathing, dignified children of God crying out for justice and opportunity. They seek not charity but a chance, not sympathy but empathy, not pity but respect.

In the course of *Think and Act Anew*, Father Snyder offers this unexpected and powerfully sensible observation on the difference between temporary assistance to those in need—hugely necessary but not sufficient—and efforts to lift the poor from dependency altogether. "The highest form of charity is not a handout but a loan," he writes. "Extending a loan treats the recipient as a peer who participates in this transaction by the promise of repayment. The individual's dignity is respected with no danger of subservience or dependency." Is this a liberal or a conservative thought, a "left" idea or "right" idea? To ask the question is to see immediately how irrelevant it is. But how many people are even thinking now of the importance of providing the poorest among us not just with incomes but also with capital? How often have we heard voices trying to blame our recent economic catastrophe on the efforts of the less well-off to acquire property by way of distracting attention from market manipulations that left the most financially privileged with millions or even billions in the bank?

Yet Father Snyder does not give up on capitalism. Instead, he proposes innovative ways of allowing the entrepreneurial spirit to flourish among the millions of Americans who have no access to board rooms or loan officers. At the same time, he emphasizes—as Catholic social thinkers always have—the essential role played by labor unions in allowing workers to bargain for decent wages and to secure some autonomy and independence in their work. Again we see the balance of the Catholic Third Way, which acknowledges both labor and capital, even as it asserts— as Pope John Paul never tired of noting—the priority of labor.

In *The Other America*, published nearly fifty years ago, the late Michael Harrington insisted that we not avert our eyes from the millions in our midst who are poor. Father Snyder has issued that urgent call again, and he, like Harrington, tells the stories of people who cannot afford nutritious food for themselves and their families, who cannot pay their utility bills, whose children are not adequately clothed, and who do not have the resources (or the insurance) to see a doctor.

But for Father Snyder, as it was for Harrington, the poor are not an undifferentiated mass, and he observes rightly that the poor in one generation do not necessarily resemble the poor in another. "The face of the poor is not the same today as it was in generations past," Father Snyder writes. "Recognizing who the poor are today is the first step to understanding the problem and finding the solution." Good intentions unmoored from knowledge and understanding can have unintended consequences. It is a problem that Father Snyder understands better than most, because of the work he does every day in Catholic Charities, an organization that is at once profoundly Catholic and profoundly American.

Catholic Charities reflects the distinctively communitarian side of Catholicism with its commitment to both solidarity and subsidiarity. Solidarity teaches us of our obligations to each other and underscores the extent to which we are embedded in a network (this might be seen as a high-tech name for the "mystical body of Christ") that binds each of us to all of us. "It is not," Pope John Paul II said, "a feeling of vague compassion or shallow distress at the misfortunes of so many people, both near and far. On the contrary, it is a firm and persevering determination to commit oneself to the common good."

Subsidiarity teaches us that the aid and social action is best carried out close to the ground. If centralization cannot always be avoided, it should be a choice of last resort. Michael Lacey and William Shea offered a rather jaunty definition of "subsidiarity" in *Commonweal* some years ago: "It can be understood minimally to say: Ask for help when you need it, give when asked, but don't spoil yourself (or anyone else), take care of your own business, and don't be an intrusive busybody." Good advice, and advice that Catholic Charities follows, one might say, religiously.

But Catholic Charities is also in an American tradition that sees independent groups in civil society as essential to problem solving, sometimes alone, sometimes in alliance with other private social action and charitable agencies, and sometimes in partnership with government. As Tocqueville observed, we are a nation that, upon seeing a problem, quickly forms an organization (or, more often, many organizations) to try to solve it. Note the founding date of Catholic Charities—1910, smack in the middle of the Progressive Era. It was a time of innovation in government—of the reforming presidencies of Theodore Roosevelt and Woodrow Wilson—but also of innovation in the sphere of what Robert Putnam, the great student of these matters, has called "social capital." As Putnam observed in a 1996 article:

> If you look at the dates at which they were created, almost all of the major civic institutions of the United States today— the Red Cross, the YWCA, the Boy Scouts, the NAACP, the Urban League, many labor unions, the Sons of Italy, the Sons of Norway, parent teacher associations, the Rotary Club, the Sierra Club, the Knights of Columbus and many others—almost all of them were formed between 1880 and 1910, an astonishingly concentrated period. We had a social capital deficit as a country created by great technological and economic change, and at that point we could have said, "Whoa, wait a minute, stop! Everybody back to the farm. It was much nicer there. We knew everybody." And similarly today we could say, "It was much nicer back in the '50s. Would all women please report to the kitchen and turn off the TV on the way?" But that is not what I am suggesting we should do. I am suggesting the contrary.
>
> Our responsibility now is to create. It is not to complain about what has happened to all the Elks Clubs or bowling leagues, but to be as socially inventive as those people a century ago who created the Red Cross, the Boy Scouts and the PTA.

Catholic Charities was part of that social effervescence a century ago, and it has endured because it continues to be creative. It is not a top-down group that imposes one social service model. It practices what it preaches by embodying subsidiarity, supporting and working with scores of independent organizations as well as government. Its partnerships encourage innovation across organizations—and within government itself.

There is a dangerous tendency in our debates about poverty to suggest that our emphasis must be either on personal responsibility or on social responsibility, that we must either ascribe poverty to individual failures or insist that all poverty is caused by social and economic injustices. But what both common sense and the Church teach is that personal responsibility and social responsibility are indivisible—indeed, that social responsibility and charity are a personal responsibility. "We must see clearly," Father Snyder writes, "that the eradication of poverty is a personal, moral mandate for each of us." And it is foolish to deny either the individual's moral obligation to the improvement of self and family or our collective obligation to break down barriers to advancement, to battle discrimination, and to dismantle unjust social structures. Social justice requires both individual and collective action.

It is impossible to discuss justice in a Catholic context without noting that the Church itself has been wracked by injustices of its own, none more searing or enraging than the child abuse scandal. For some, it is very hard to think about Catholicism without thinking about the scandal. The Church's handling of episodes in which the young and the innocent suffered grievously at the hands of those in authority drove many away and enraged millions of others who have struggled to remain faithful.

The Church still needs to come to terms with the impact of the scandal and to grapple forthrightly with its own institutional failures. But it will thrive again if it remembers the lessons Father Snyder teaches here about its larger mission and its obligation to speak not to a narrow set of questions but to its largest obligations to society, to humanity, and to God.

It has also helped many Catholics to remember that the Church is more than a few leaders. In a powerful column in *The New York Times*, Nicholas Kristof spoke of a "grass-roots Catholic Church that does far more good in the world than it ever gets credit for."

> This is the church [he wrote] that supports extraordinary aid organizations like Catholic Relief Services and Caritas, saving lives every day, and that operates superb schools that provide needy children an escalator out of poverty.
>
> This is the church of the nuns and priests in Congo, toiling in obscurity to feed and educate children. . . .
>
> This is the church of the Maryknoll Sisters in Central America and the Cabrini Sisters in Africa. . . .

And this is the Church of Catholic Charities—and of the social mission to which Father Snyder calls us all.

June 30, 2010

Preface

From the beginnings of the Catholic Charities movement in America, our agencies have recognized their dual mission to serve the poor and advocate for effective social policies to eradicate the causes of poverty. We are called by Scripture, the wisdom of our tradition and leadership of the Church, and Catholic social teaching to raise our voices for the common good, speaking with and on behalf of the vulnerable. We are called to be architects—to partner with others to rebuild our society and nation on a framework of justice. These roles took on a new imperative in 2008, when the global economic crisis thrust millions of Americans out of work and into our centers—families, single parents, children, and grandparents seeking such basics as housing, shelter, and food.

Recognizing that we were experiencing a sea change in the poverty landscape in America, Catholic Charities USA convened a series of regional leadership forums around the country in 2009 and 2010 to tap the expertise and ideas for reducing poverty from those most familiar with it—Catholic Charities services providers and other community leaders. From the first meeting in St. Paul, Minnesota, groups met in Portland, Oregon; San Antonio, Texas; San Jose, California; Atlanta, Georgia; Albany, New York; Nashville, Tennessee; Cleveland, Ohio; Chicago, Illinois; and Newark, New Jersey. The issues continued to be explored via the online forum, "Big Ideas: 21st Century Solutions to Poverty Forum," where "big ideas" to reduce poverty were posted and discussed. I began a blog, "Think and Act Anew," to engage a broader group of people in the discussion.

This book is an attempt to capture many of the ideas from

those meetings and forums and use them to ignite a national discussion as we seek to rebuild our economy to ensure that it includes everyone.

This book is not intended to be a scholarly work but represents the urgency that we feel to ensure that the situation and needs of soaring numbers of people affected by the adverse economy are taken into account as solutions are proposed and adopted. As such it is a book very much "written while running" and may reflect some of the frenetic activity rooted in the need to act in a timely fashion. My apologies for any unintentional oversight, but I am convinced that the lives of many children and families depend on our doing the right thing on their behalf at this time in our history. Such a context begs for your open mind and understanding and my gratitude for such.

Acknowledgments

This book is grounded in the daily work of the thousands of dedicated people who serve the poor and marginalized every day at Catholic Charities agencies throughout this country. I am humbled and honored to share that mission with them. I am grateful to work with a creative and passionate staff at the national office who are leaders in making the voice of the poor heard in Washington and in supporting our local members.

But in a special way, I am grateful to Monsignor J. Jerome Boxleitner, my mentor, who led Catholic Charities in the Twin Cities for almost forty years. He taught us all that walking with our God means walking with the poor. He will never know the lives that have been impacted for the better by his diligence and sometimes stubbornness. I have been blessed to work so closely with a visionary and icon in the Catholic Charities movement.

Finally, I wish to thank Susan Perry and the staff of Orbis Books for believing that this project would make a positive contribution to the public discourse surrounding the needs of the poor and our collective response. Many hands have sufficed for what two would not have been able to do alone. My sincere thanks!

May God who has begun this great work in us bring it to fruition.

Reflections on *Caritas in Veritate*

Love in truth — *caritas in veritate* — is a great challenge for the Church in a world that is becoming progressively and pervasively globalized. The risk for our time is that the *de facto* interdependence of people and nations is not matched by ethical interaction of consciences and minds that would give rise to truly human development. Only *in charity, illumined by the light of reason and faith*, is it possible to pursue development goals that possess a more humane and humanizing value. The sharing of goods and resources, from which authentic development proceeds, is not guaranteed by merely technical progress and relationships of utility, but by the potential of love that overcomes evil with good (cf. Rom 12:21), opening up the path towards reciprocity of consciences and liberties.

The Church does not have technical solutions to offer and does not claim "to interfere in any way in the politics of States." She does, however, have a mission of truth to accomplish, in every time and circumstance, for a society that is attuned to man, to his dignity, to his vocation. Without truth, it is easy to fall into an empiricist and sceptical view of life, incapable of rising to the level of praxis because of a lack of interest in grasping the values — sometimes even the meanings — with which to judge and direct it. Fidelity to man requires *fidelity to the truth*, which alone is the *guarantee of freedom* (cf. Jn 8:32) and of *the possibility of integral human development*. For this reason the Church searches for truth, proclaims it tirelessly and recognizes it wherever it is manifested. This mission of truth is something that the

Church can never renounce. Her social doctrine is a particular dimension of this proclamation: it is a service to the truth which sets us free. Open to the truth, from whichever branch of knowledge it comes, the Church's social doctrine receives it, assembles into a unity the fragments in which it is often found, and mediates it within the constantly changing life-patterns of the society of peoples and nations (Benedict XVI, *Caritas in Veritate*, 9).

Caritas in Veritate, or Charity in Truth, Pope Benedict XVI's third encyclical, deals with social justice. By "charity" he means a form of self-giving and other-regarding love, not simply giving to those in need. The encyclical was issued in July 2009 at the height of the global economic crisis. Drawing on moral wisdom and upon the Gospel message of Jesus as proclaimed by the Church, he challenges everyone to embrace "charity in truth" and to confront the social challenges we face today.

Caritas in Veritate is the inspiration for this book. With all possible humility I intend to follow the path marked out by Benedict XVI and apply his teachings to the circumstances in which we find ourselves in the United States.

Chapter 1
Rebuilding an America for Everyone

One evening a man gathered his closest friends and associates and told them stories of the end of this world and the coming of the next. He ended with a story of the king of the next world who would gather all people before him and separate them into the righteous and the unrighteous:

> Then the king will say to those at his right hand, "Come, you that are blessed by my Father, inherit the kingdom prepared for you from the foundation of the world; for I was hungry and you gave me food, I was thirsty and you gave me something to drink, I was a stranger and you welcomed me, I was naked and you gave me clothing, I was sick and you took care of me, I was in prison and you visited me." Then the righteous will answer him, "Lord, when was it that we saw you hungry and gave you food, or thirsty and gave you something to drink? And when was it that we saw you a stranger and welcomed you, or naked and gave you clothing? And when was it that we saw you sick or in prison and visited you?" And the king will answer them, "Truly I tell you, just as you did it to one of the least of these who are members of my family, you did it to me" (Matt. 25:32-40).

Of course this man was Jesus Christ. He was sitting on the Mount of Olives, two days before his arrest and execution on the cross. His friends and associates were the disciples who went on to found a religion and build a church based on his life, his death and resurrection, and his commandments.

The Gospel Challenge and America's Poor

In this small book I ask Americans to make new and different efforts to treat the least among us as sisters and brothers of Christ.

I mean this as a transforming call to real action, not simply tinkering around the edges of old approaches. And we have a real opportunity now, as we rebuild America out of the ashes of the bank failures and mortgage foreclosures and job losses of the past few years. I firmly believe that as we rebuild we can also cut poverty in half in America by the year 2020.

This will not be easy, but it is well within our God-given abilities and our God-given resources.

Reducing poverty and ensuring that all the remaining poor live with dignity will require that we reconsider all our old ways of thinking about the poor and how to help them. We have been doing certain things for the poor in certain ways for generations, even centuries. Have those things and ways ever actually succeeded? Did they succeed under older circumstances but are not up to the task in today's world? Are there better ways available with today's technologies or other resources? Do we ourselves, or others among us, have vested interests in poverty, or in ways of treating the poor?

I think we can create a new vision of America in 2020. And, beginning today, we can build that America.

This book speaks from and about the bitter truths of our recent and current experience. The housing-based financial bubble that burst quickly drove this country, and indeed the world, to the brink of a second Great Depression. Rapid and controversial actions by Presidents Bush and Obama and their administrations in 2008 and 2009 appear to have staved off that disaster, but the recession has been broad and deep, and as of this writing in mid-2010 the recovery has been slow and fitful.

The numbers of the poor, measured in the way America has

measured poverty for fifty years, have increased dramatically. Almost forty million Americans are poor. Unemployment remains near 10 percent, with nearly fifteen million of our people without jobs. Unemployment is likely to remain high for a long time, and many people have given up hope of ever having a secure job.

From 2007 to 2009 the number of people that Catholic Charities agencies across the country serve rose by 16.4 percent to nearly 9.25 million people. More fundamentally, who the poor and those at risk of poverty are, why they are poor or at risk of poverty, and what their prospects are for leaving or avoiding poverty—all this has changed.

These hard times are also an opportunity and a call to reconsider what we believe in and to determine how we can return America to much deeper values—the ones Jesus Christ taught the disciples—even as we move forward.

In 2009 Pope Benedict XVI issued an encyclical—a formal letter to the entire Church—entitled *Caritas in Veritate*, Charity in Truth. *Caritas in Veritate*, as I read it, is a call to and a road map for rebuilding the global economy so that we don't forget "the least of these," so that we love our neighbors as ourselves.

Pope Benedict urges all nations to rebuild their economies in a way that works toward the common good and the real needs of our neighbors. The Holy Father reminds us of the Gospel mandate to practice charity. He challenges business enterprises, governments, unions, and individuals to reexamine their economic responsibilities in the light of charity governed by truth in society. I will refer frequently in this book to *Caritas in Veritate* as I discuss different aspects of the challenge of rebuilding an America that does not tolerate poverty and that provides opportunities for everyone, including the least among us.

This is more than an effort to invoke the Holy Father's authority. I ask all American Catholics, and indeed all people of faith and all other readers, to read *Caritas in Veritate* and to take seriously Benedict's analysis of where the human family finds itself today. We need to examine how we got here so that we might determine how we need to change the way in which we move forward.

"*Caritas in Veritate* is the principle around which the church's social doctrine turns," Pope Benedict XVI notes as he considers two criteria that govern moral action, "*justice and the common good*" (*Caritas in Veritate*, 6). He continues:

> *Charity goes beyond justice*, because to love is to give, to offer what is "mine" to the other; but it never lacks justice, which prompts us to give the other what is "his," what is due to him by reason of his being or his acting. I cannot "give" what is mine to the other, without first giving him what pertains to him in justice. If we love others with charity, then first of all we are just towards them. . . . [J]ustice is inseparable from charity, and intrinsic to it. Justice is the primary way of charity or, in Paul VI's words, "the minimum measure of it. . . . [C]harity demands justice: recognition and respect for the legitimate rights of individuals and peoples. It strives to build the *earthly city* according to law and justice (*Caritas in Veritate*, 6).

Benedict tells us that every Christian is called to this charity. I would extend this mandate to all Americans, if not based on the encyclical, then on the promises of our nation's founders. The centrality of the human person in society was boldly declared by our nation's founders in the United States Declaration of Independence:

> We hold these truths to be self-evident: That all men are created equal; that they are endowed by their Creator with

certain unalienable rights; that among these are life, liberty, and the pursuit of happiness; that, to secure these rights, governments are instituted among men, deriving their just powers from the consent of the governed . . . (*United States Declaration of Independence*, July 4, 1776).

In America today we may believe that all men and women are equal, but this is not enough. We must embrace a more urgent mandate—that life is sacred. Life comes from God, it belongs to God, it returns to God. All human beings are not only created equal, they have equal dignity. We exercise our love of God by desiring each person's good, as well as the common good, or, as it is expressed in the Constitution of the United States of America, by promoting the general welfare.

I don't think anyone will disagree that the general welfare was not a priority for the individuals and organizations that took untold financial risks for the purpose of amassing wealth. As David Leonhardt noted in *The New York Times*, there is plenty of blame to go around for the current recession, but much of it comes from an attitude that "confused the fact that market capitalism was the best economic system with the misguided notion that it was the perfect system" (Robert J. Barbara as quoted in Leonhardt's "Crossroads: Theory and Morality in the New Economy," August 23, 2009).

Innovative thought alone will not be enough to bring about the changes that are needed. In his 2009 encyclical Pope Benedict emphasizes that the cause of our failures goes deeper "than lack of deep thought; it is 'the lack of brotherhood among individuals and peoples'" (*Caritas in Veritate*, 19). He explains:

Will it ever be possible to obtain this brotherhood by human effort alone? As society becomes ever more globalized, it makes us neighbors but does not make us brothers. Reason, by itself, is capable of grasping the equality between men and of giving stability to their civic coexistence, but it cannot establish fraternity. This originates in a transcendent vocation from God the Father, who loved us first, teaching us through the Son what fraternal charity is (*Caritas in Veritate*, 19).

As I understand the Holy Father, we can understand with our minds that we are neighbors, equals, and responsible together for the terms of our lives in society, but to succeed in acting anew, in transforming our lives together, we must answer Christ's call to share as one family, brothers and sisters, in the love of Christ and the life of God.

How the Church Is Responding

Catholic Charities is attempting to answer that call. In 2009 and through 2010 we began a year-long effort to unearth the root causes of poverty in America. We set out to tap the expertise and vision of those who know American poverty and American resources the best—the providers of Catholic Charities services and other community leaders and organizations. We held regional leadership forums in the ten cities noted in the Preface with representatives from each region of the country. Panels of local experts addressed the most compelling needs in their areas and why we need to heed a call to action. Others presented creative ideas that work to encourage local initiatives to solve local problems.

We then took the initial insights and possibilities to the broader public, encouraging collaboration through wiki technology on our "Big Ideas: 21st Century Solutions to Poverty Forum," and through my blog "Think and Act Anew" (http://www.thinkandactanew.org/).

The successful programs we encountered and the ideas that were generated will be described throughout this book.

One distinctive feature of the American people that I find encouraging is our willingness to experiment—to try something, and if it does not work out to try something else. Or, if we find something that does work, to scale it up. FDR's New Deal was a series of federal experiments, and we have learned in recent years to let states and local governments experiment as well.

It is in the very best tradition of American Catholicism to take a leadership role in these American efforts at self-transformation. During the Great Depression, Monsignor John O'Grady, the second General Secretary of the National Conference of Catholic Charities (Catholic Charities USA), who was one of the leaders of the Catholic social movement, insisted on professionalism in our services and strengthening our local diocesan agencies. He and the founding leader of Catholic Charities, Monsignor William Kerby, played a significant role in developing the Social Security Act of 1935, undoubtedly the greatest anti-poverty government program this country has ever created.

In his memoirs Monsignor O'Grady chronicles the immense challenges faced by the Catholic Charities movement of his time. In 1910 when Monsignor Kerby founded Catholic Charities USA, over half of the Catholics in this country were born in foreign lands. As they came to these shores they overtaxed the social welfare system and the child welfare system, as well as the penal system. Then when thousands of young men returned from World War I, they faced an economy without jobs to offer them. The final blow came when the giant bubble of financial speculation burst, creating a tidal wave of poverty in its wake.

The leadership of the founding generation of Catholic Charities did not look around at this suffering nation for signs of hope. Instead, they set out to be the signs of hope. And they succeeded. We can do no less.

Archbishop John Ireland was a leader in my home archdiocese of St. Paul through the turn of the twentieth century. On the occasion of the centennial of the establishment of the hierarchy in the United States in 1889, he addressed all the country's bishops. After an earlier speaker had pointed out the wonderful things accomplished in the first hundred years, Archbishop Ireland said,

> I bid you turn to the future. It has special significance for us. The past our fathers wrought; the future will be wrought by us. The next century . . . will be what we make it. It will be our own, the work of our labors. O for a prophet's eye to glance down the unborn years, and from now to read the story . . . as generations a hundred years hence may read it. But no prophet's eye is needed. As we will it, so shall the story be.

As we will it, so shall the future be.

Chapter 2
The Faces of the Poor Are Familiar

And she gave birth to her firstborn son and wrapped him in bands of cloth, and laid him in a manger, because there was no place for them in the inn (Luke 2:7).

Jesus declared his solidarity with the poor by being born as one of them, not as King of Kings, heir to David's throne, in palatial surroundings, but in a humble stable. We have all witnessed this scene being played out in children's Christmas pageants—the infant Son of God, in a bed of straw, visited by angels and by shepherds with their flocks.

Some thirty years later, Jesus climbed a mountain, sat down, and spoke to the people gathered there who had followed him, delivering what we now call the Sermon on the Mount from the Gospel of Matthew. This includes the Beatitudes, beginning with "Blessed are the poor in spirit, for theirs is the kingdom of heaven" (Matt. 5:3). Although Matthew focuses on the spiritual dimension of poverty, in the Gospel of Luke this same Beatitude begins, "Blessed are the poor, for theirs is the kingdom of heaven."

The Catholic tradition of social teaching understands this particular blessing to include economic need and distress, the whole of the painful condition of the poor, their low position in society—their dependence on the social network around them, and their defenseless exposure to injustice. Later, in the Parable of the Last Judgment from the Gospel of Matthew (cited in chapter 1), Jesus turns these ideas into action: feed the hungry, give the thirsty something to drink, provide hospitality to strangers, clothe the naked, take care of the sick and imprisoned.

Though this list of the works or acts was later formalized as the Corporal Works of Mercy, the importance of performing these duties has been urged from the earliest days of the Church. They stem from living according to Christ's declaration of the greatest commandment in the Gospel of Matthew:

> He said to him, "You shall love the Lord your God with all your heart, and with all your soul, and with all your mind." This is the greatest and first commandment. And a second is like it: "You shall love your neighbor as yourself." On these two commandments hang all the law and the prophets (Matt. 22:37-40).

These commandments, thousands of years old, help to form the basis of Catholic social action. All of us are to have compassion for, and, if possible, to alleviate another's misfortune. It is from these teachings that Catholic Charities began.

Catholic Charities traces its roots back to 1727, almost fifty years before the thirteen original colonies in America issued their Declaration of Independence from Great Britain. In the early eighteenth century, when the French Ursuline Sisters opened an orphanage in New Orleans in what was then New France, they also established a school, a hospital, and outreach to "women working on the streets," or prostitutes. Other Catholic institutions were established in major cities along the East Coast, providing homes and education for children whose parents were lost to disease and tragedies common in early America.

With the rise of immigration in the mid-1800s, the demand for Catholic charitable outreach increased dramatically. By the early twentieth century when the Church was still overwhelm-

A New Form of Poverty

In March of 2004, Alicia and her husband planned to build a truck-driving business in Tucson, with her husband as the owner-operator. They sold their home and bought another with enough space for their big rig and flatbed. Later they realized their loan's terms called for monthly mortgage payments that kept increasing. Then came high fuel costs and road taxes.

Unable to make ends meet, their home was foreclosed on and their nightmare began. They sold all of their possessions—furniture, toys, clothes, everything. Alicia and the children moved in with her parents. Her husband felt like a failure to his family.

Eventually, Catholic Community Services Pio Decimo Center in Tuscon, Arizona, put the family into transitional housing, found a job for Alicia, while her husband found work driving for a transportation service for people with disabilities. They are working hard to restore their credit rating.

Alicia says, "Having your own home should not come as a result of loans that, in the end, are not affordable. We know we are not alone with our experience so we MUST come together and unite to ask for the opportunities that reward hard work and doing the right things. I plan to be part of that solution and I believe we all have a chance to make a difference NOW."

ingly made up of foreign-born members and also predominantly poor, a Catholic Charities network had developed to provide social services and health care and serve as an advocate for the poor.

Today, the Catholic Charities network includes more than 1,700 agencies across the United States—one of the nation's largest social service networks, with 240,000 compassionate volunteers, staff, and board members serving 9.25 million people.

In recent years, however, the faces of the poor who come to the doors of our offices throughout the country have been changing, while their numbers have been steadily growing. Poverty is no longer hidden away in urban pockets or in remote rural areas. In this new economic reality, poverty surrounds us everywhere, from the cities to the suburbs to rural America.

Some of the many misconceptions about the nature of poverty in the United States reinforce the commonly held view that poverty is due to the failures and deficiencies of individuals, rather than the failures of structures that we put in place through the economic and political choices we make as a nation. While it is true that individual choices and behaviors do influence one's chances of living in poverty, these individual behaviors are frequently outweighed by the structures and policies that shape the opportunities of people who are poor.

The great American tradition has been that if you work hard you can provide a better life for yourself and your family. This is the bedrock of the "American Dream." Unfortunately, too many Americans today are working very hard but still cannot make ends meet.

More than half of Americans will experience poverty for at least one year.

What is perhaps most frightening is that poverty is expanding into nearly all segments of society. Mark R. Rank, a professor in the School of Social Work at Washington University and a noted researcher on poverty, has estimated some of the risks of experiencing poverty. He writes:

[B]eginning at age 20, 31 percent of Americans will have

experienced at least one year of poverty by the time they reach age 35, 45 percent will have done so by age 55, and 59 percent will encounter a year or more of poverty by age 75. In addition, 68 percent of Americans will experience a year below 125 percent of the poverty line between the ages of 20 and 75, and 76 percent of Americans will face a year below 150 percent of the poverty line.

He concludes from these staggering numbers that "What these percentages strikingly reveal is that rather than being an event that affects a small minority of the U.S. population, poverty is a mainstream experience that touches a clear majority of Americans at some point during their adult lifetimes."[1]

Who Are the Poor?

A study by the AARP Policy Institute indicates that close to one in ten older adults (those sixty-five and over) live in poverty, and half again as many live just above the poverty threshold, based on the 2008 federal poverty threshold of $10,326 for single elderly persons.[2]

The men and women who serve our country are not immune. One social worker noted on our online forum that some of the homeless are Vietnam veterans. Many did not receive adequate care for the mental, physical, or spiritual damage they suffered from when they returned from the war, and were "left with no limbs and nothing to live for."

And, today, having a job does not preclude living in poverty. Two out of three families with incomes below the poverty level have at least one member who is employed.[3]

Millions of others do not fall below the official federal poverty levels, but they are asset-poor and are at risk of falling into poverty in the event of a single emergency such as the situation

The experiences of Catholic Charities agencies are well supported by the numbers presented in U.S. Census data, independent research studies, and the media.

Almost half of all people living in poverty, about 47 percent, are white and non-Hispanic. However, African Americans and Hispanics are much more likely to live in poverty than other population groups.

The number of Hispanics living in poverty is now about the same as the number of African Americans living in poverty.

17 million households, or 14.6 percent, in our nation had trouble putting food on the table in 2008, an increase from 13 million, or 11.1 percent of households in 2007. Food banks saw a 30 percent increase in the number of people served in 2009.[4]

African Americans, Latino Americans, and Native Americans are about three times as likely to live in poverty as are whites.

In 2008, 16.3 percent of Americans living in rural areas were poor, but they accounted for 33 percent of the total increase in the number of poor Americans from 2003 to 2008 —more than one million people.[5]

When it comes to children, the poverty rates for different ethnic groups vary widely, but can range from 10 percent for white children, and as high as 33 percent for children of color.

for the residents of New Orleans in the wake of Hurricane Katrina, or those whose livelihoods have been impacted for an unforeseeable time by the expansive oil spill in the Gulf of Mexico.

These are the working poor, including, for example, the people who prepare and serve food at many fast food restaurants who make an average of $8.60 per hour, or $17,888 yearly. Their income falls $4,162 below the federal poverty level.[6] The poverty guideline in 2009 for a family of four was $22,050. To surpass the poverty guideline for a family of four, a worker would need to earn an hourly wage of at least $10.60 (full-time, year round).[7] Compare this to the national minimum wage, which in 2010 is $7.25.

Many families of soldiers fighting in Iraq and Afghanistan are using more food stamps than in previous years. In 2008, according to an article in the military news section of a website (www.military.com) devoted to helping "the 30 million Americans with military affinity stay connected and informed," soldiers and their families redeemed food stamps "at nearly twice the civilian rate, according to Defense Commissary Agency figures." That government agency reported

that more than $31 million worth of food stamps were used at commissaries nationwide in 2008—an increase of about $6.2 million, or more than 25 percent—from the $24.8 million redeemed in 2007. That contrasts with a 13 percent overall increase in food stamp use by Americans for the same period, according to the Department of Agriculture, which administers the food stamp program.[8]

One Catholic Charities worker realized not long ago that she and her brother grew up poor but never thought about it at the time because of the way their mother worked continuously, every day of the week for years, to feed, house, and clothe them. "Many people do not recognize that they are impoverished," she said, "because they don't know any other way of living." In her case they were given an avenue to improve their situation—both joined the military, became educated, and went on to successful careers.

The New Poor

The economic crisis our country currently is experiencing has had a devastating impact on the lives of millions of other

Americans who have lost their jobs or their homes and who struggle each and every day, often holding out hope of regaining employment in the near future. On top of the difficulties of not having the resources to sustain themselves and their families in the downturn, many must deal with problems of lowered self-esteem. *The New York Times* reported that in 2009 nearly one in five Americans said that at some point during the year they did not have enough money to buy the food they needed, and that "more than 38 million Americans—one in eight—now receive food stamps, a record high." The same *New York Times* article also reported that the most recent data (for 2008) from the Agriculture Department's annual survey of "food insecurity," "found that 14.6 percent of Americans lacked consistent access to sufficient food, the highest in the survey's fourteen-year history."[9]

According to the Census Bureau, by September 2009, 39.8 million people were living in poverty in the United States. There are now 15 million unemployed. The numbers served by Catholic Charities agencies across the country grew by three-quarters of a million people in 2009 alone, a 16.4 percent increase from 2007 when the recession began.

It is hard to believe that as recently as February 2008 the national unemployment rate in the United States was 4.8 percent. A year later unemployment had almost doubled, and it continued to climb until it reached 10.1 percent in October 2009.[10] It has declined only slightly since then.

These are the new poor in America. Their faces are familiar to us because we know them. They can be our neighbors, or family, or friends.

A CBS News report in September 2009 told the story of a 56-year-old lifelong construction worker from Little Rock, Arkansas, who receives food stamps. He hasn't had regular work for months since many jobs dried up in the housing meltdown.

He worries about getting sick or injured because he doesn't know whether he could cover the medical expenses. Now working a part-time, minimum-wage job, he said it doesn't matter to him how the poverty numbers are sliced so long as people get a fair shake at getting assistance. He said, "I often tell my son, 'You've got to save your money. Live within your means because you never know when things might take a turn.'"[11]

Despite a series of extensions in unemployment benefits, hundreds of thousands of workers have depleted their savings as they struggle to keep their homes and feed their families while looking for work.[12]

In April 2010, the number of unemployed persons was 15.3 million; the number of long-term unemployed reached 6.7 million, and 45.9 percent of unemployed persons had been jobless for 27 weeks or more. According to the AARP, unemployment among Americans ages 55 | increased 331 percent over the last ten years.[13]

Many of those jobs are not coming back. Manufacturing sectors are shrinking or disappearing outright. *The Wall Street Journal* reported in May of this year that only once since 1948 has the U.S. shed manufacturing capacity on a net basis, and never by as much as it has recently.[14]

Just as disturbing is what we read in a February 2010 article in *The New York Times*. It is as insightful as it is alarming.

Economists fear that the nascent recovery will leave more people behind than in past recessions, failing to create jobs in sufficient numbers to absorb the record-setting ranks of the long-term unemployed. Call them the new poor: people long accustomed to the comforts of middle-class life who are now relying on public assistance for the first time in their lives—potentially for years to come. . . . Every downturn pushes some people out of the middle class before the economy resumes expanding. Most recover. Many prosper. But some economists worry that this time could be different. An unusual constellation of forces—some embedded in the modern-day economy, others unique to this wrenching recession—might make it especially difficult for those out of work to find their way back to their middle-class lives.[15]

This is not news to anyone on the frontlines of Catholic Charities agencies or other social service providers who make up the safety net of this country. Quarterly snapshot surveys of our member agencies have presented a picture of continued and growing need since 2008.

Our First Quarter 2010 Snapshot Survey, which is first-hand data from the Catholic Charities agencies that provide services to those in need every day, revealed a dramatic increase nationwide in requests for life-sustaining emergency services.

The survey painted a vivid picture of the new American middle class. Of the agencies responding to the survey, 75 percent reported an increase in families seeking assistance, 72 percent reported an increase in the working poor seeking assistance, 61 percent reported an increase in the middle class seeking assistance, and 58 percent reported an increase in the homeless seeking assistance.

"We've Never Had to Ask for Help Before"

Despite news that the recession might be subsiding, for many the crisis is only beginning. The staff and volunteers at Catholic Charities agencies throughout the country continue to see new faces coming to their doors every day. There were startling increases in the number of working, middle-class families in need of emergency food and assistance with utility/rent/mortgage payments. There were also significant increases in requests for counseling and mental health services—certainly understandable as families worry how they will feed their children, find a job that pays a living wage, or avoid foreclosure of their mortgage.

In Yakima, Washington, it is becoming common for social workers to hear the phrase: "We've never had to ask for help like this before."[16] Because of the increased requests for assistance, one Catholic Charities agency that provides clothing and housewares for those in need has been forced to enact a new policy in which walk-in emergency assistance is available only once instead of every six months.

Our agencies have longer waiting lists and more people who would be considered middle class asking for help. The executive director of one, referring to her clients, noted, "There is a certain desperation that you can hear in their voices."[17]

We are seeing more working families, more single parents, and more grandparents seeking such basics services as housing, shelter, and food. Too many of these families are just holding on and are struggling to make ends meet.

The existence of such widespread and long-term poverty amidst such enormous wealth as we experience in the United States is a moral and social wound on the soul of our country. The harm it inflicts on our entire nation continues to grow.

The fact that this powerful economy leaves so many behind is a sign that something in our social and economic system is seriously broken. Unlike natural disasters such as hurricanes and floods, poverty in the United States is a human-made disaster. It is not a force of nature beyond our control; rather, it is the result of economic, social, and political choices that we Americans have made, both as individuals and as a society.

Catholic teaching asserts that one of the principal means by which society and the state can and must defend human dignity is by giving priority to the needs of the poor. We now know who they are. The faces of the poor are familiar to us—perhaps our neighbors, friends, members of our parish, or relatives—and each one is the face of Christ.

Defining Poverty

One Catholic Charities director has asked: How can we define poverty in America so that people might determine if they are indeed poor? Can we make this somehow measurable? He suggests that someone is poor if:

1. They cannot afford housing that is clean, safe, and in good repair.

2. They cannot afford nutritious food for themselves and their family on a regular basis.

3. They cannot consistently pay their utility bills even though it is a priority.

4. Their children are not adequately clothed for school with clean clothes that fit and are in good repair, and they do not have proper clothing for work.

5. They cannot afford to go to the doctor for any kind of illness for fear that the visit will be beyond their means to pay for it.

All of the above factors take into account that a person is trying to do the very best he or she can do and still cannot succeed. The face of the poor is not the same today as it was in generations past. Recognizing who the poor are today is the first step to understanding the problem and finding a solution.

Chapter 3
The Dignity and Importance of Each Person

On a beautiful sunny summer morning in Minneapolis, a man decided to go for a placid walk around the Lake of the Isles. It was one of those perfect days that makes putting up with winter in Minnesota bearable. As he walked around the lake and contemplated the goodness of life, the stillness around him was abruptly interrupted by someone in the middle of the lake splashing and yelling and carrying on wildly. Perturbed at this rude interruption, the man yelled out to the person in the lake: "Why are you carrying on like this and disturbing everyone's peace?" The answer came back: "I can't swim! I can't swim!" The morning walker replied: "Well, neither can I, but you don't see me disturbing everyone else!"

There is quite a disconnect between the two people in this story. To the person who is safe and secure on the shore, the one who is splashing and yelling in the lake is simply an irritation or interruption during a placid walk. He does not see that perhaps there is a greater connection between them than a chance encounter on a summer morning. He does not recognize that the person drowning is his neighbor in need, or, to put it more accurately, his brother or sister.

In a similar vein, I am amazed at news stories of people going to heroic efforts to save an animal in danger, while on the next page is a story of someone being robbed or worse while several people simply walk by. I wonder if the collective quality of life of pets in the United States is higher than the collective quality of life of children. If so, how could that be?

Now, before anyone reports me to the ASPCA, let me say

that I am an avid animal lover who is convinced that they are a special gift given to us by God at creation. But why is it sometimes easier to make a connection with an animal in need than it is with a human being in need? But that is not what I would like to address in this chapter. The point of the story that will occupy my thoughts is the relationship between the two people—between any two people. For whether we like it or not, we are intricately bound to each other in a relationship that transcends human choice or even familial ties. Consequently, all of our decisions ultimately have an impact on the lives of others and must be weighed as such, not only as individuals but, just as important, as a society.

I have heard the question asked—many times over, actually—why Catholic Charities USA has the audacity to address the issue of poverty in the United States in an authoritative way. I also know that there are questions surrounding why Catholic Charities USA has the audacity to set a goal of reducing poverty in this country in half by the year 2020. One response is that we have credibility because in 2009 we served more than nine million people in need in a variety of ways that cover the spectrum of human services. That is roughly one in four people living in poverty in the United States. We are credible because we not only talk about reducing poverty, we are on the frontlines serving people each and every day, working to find them a path out of poverty. In this regard we are like many other nonprofit organizations that, because of their mission of service and working for the common good, contribute not only to the well-being of families and individuals, but also to the well-being and vitality of communities.

There is however a more fundamental reason that Catholic Charities and other faith-based organizations are committed to what they do day in and day out. To put it simply: we have no choice. We have no choice because there are moral prescriptions that are foundational to our faith. These moral principles mandate our work. They define not only our actions but also the actions and lives of all disciples. The next chapters will explore some of these principles that are found in Catholic social teaching in order to highlight the wisdom they offer about shaping a society that is just and compassionate.

Human Dignity—The Heart of Catholic Social Teaching

To begin, the most foundational principle of all is the dignity and value of every human being. In the first chapters of the Book of Genesis, the first book of the Hebrew Scriptures, we find an amazing account of the creation of the world. At the end of each day, God looks at what has been created and sees that it is good. (A point that we do not always remember!) But the crowning point is when God creates human beings. Genesis tells us that we are made male and female and in the image and likeness of God. This is quite a departure from other religious beliefs of that time. The images of the gods of other religions were cast out of wood or stone, and sometimes they were ferocious. In contrast to this, the image of the God that comes from Genesis is a living image buried deep within the beauty of every human being.

The meaning here is clear: every human being is worthy of dignity and respect because every human being carries within himself or herself the image and likeness of God. Therefore, the same respect and awe that should be given to God should be given to human beings—as the bearers of God's image—in a way that is different from the rest of creation. The rest of creation reflects the beauty and majesty of God and needs to be reverenced as a great gift to be experienced and enjoyed. But human beings should command a special respect that should also define our relationship with one another.

It would be difficult to overstate the importance of this principle. All of the other social principles in Catholic social teaching depend upon and flow from this foundation. The implications of this basic principle are gradually revealed throughout the rest of sacred Scripture. Our connection to each other is addressed in the following passage from the Book of Deuteronomy:

> If there is among you anyone in need, a member of your community in any of your towns within the land that the LORD your God is giving you, do not be hard-hearted or tight-fisted towards your needy neighbor. You should rather open your hand, willingly lending enough to meet the need, whatever it may be. . . . Give liberally and be ungrudging when you do so, for on this account the LORD your God will bless you in all your work and in all that you undertake. Since there will never cease to be some in need on the earth, I therefore command you, "Open your hand to the poor and needy neighbor in your land" (Deut. 15:7-8, 10-11).

In Judeo-Christian thought, generosity to our neighbor should mirror the generosity that God has shown us. This should be done freely and not with ill will. As we have been blessed, so should we be a blessing to others, opening our hearts and our hands.

In this same spirit, the Muslim tradition prescribes the giving of alms, which should be accompanied by the following greeting: "Thank you for giving me the opportunity to fulfill the obligations of my religion."

As beautiful as the creation account in Genesis is, and as clear as the directives in Deuteronomy are, in philosophy our starting point must be a Christian anthropology. If we are to have a meaningful dialogue on the importance of human beings, we need first of all to understand the underpinnings of our view of what it means to be human. Pope Benedict XVI has advised us that "the social question has become a radically anthropological question" (*Caritas in Veritate*, 75). To be sure, there are differing anthropological viewpoints from which people view reality and the world. A secular humanist situates the meaning of life in a place different from a Christian believer. While even those of different faiths may have a common core belief in the value of life and the person, how that is applied is influenced by specific beliefs about ultimate purpose, afterlife, redemption, and salvation.

For the Christian, meaning and value in life transcend appearance, what can be seen with the eyes. Our reference point is beyond ourselves. To those who say that religion or faith should be a private matter that does not enter into or influence public discourse, we respond that these core beliefs are integral to who we are and who we are called to be and cannot be segmented or compartmentalized from how we interact in the public forum. Human rights for us are rooted in human nature and not simply bestowed by the government. There are those who are insistent that the United States is a Christian nation. I am not sure if they maintain this because a majority of citizens identify themselves as Christian, or if they mean that our social policy is based on the Christian principle of human dignity and respect. If it is the latter, it would be hard to prove when one evaluates the relative priority of children or the marginalized in our public policy.

Human Dignity and the Economic Crisis

What are the implications of this foundational principle if we are to think and act anew? Such an anthropological approach would require that the principle of the dignity and value of each person have implications in every aspect of the human experience since all activity, if it is truly human, has intrinsic value. That value, endowed at creation by God, means that as individuals and as a society there are ideals that we cannot compromise. In the complexity of our ever-developing social and human experience, we cannot let our institutions outpace our ethical understandings of their impact. This has been the case recently with the collapse of some of our financial institutions, which now requires that we evaluate and redesign systems in a way that ensures that they will not bring financial harm to the very people they claim to serve.

Another important consideration is that we cannot compartmentalize human beings or the human experience by isolating aspects of our social systems from the underlying supposition that they are meant first of all to enhance the lives of human beings and not simply to improve the profit margins of shareholders. Ethics cannot be suspended from economic policies, strategies, or decisions any more than it should be disconnected from politics. All economic decisions have implications on people's lives. Again, Pope Benedict reminds us: "Purchasing is always a moral—and not simply economic—act. Hence the consumer has a specific social responsibility" (*Caritas in Veritate*, 66).

This has ramifications for us as individuals as we see more and more people's lives being adversely affected by the economy. The greed of a few has inversely affected the quality and sustainability of life for many. In a purely economic sense, our lives are affected by the loss of tax revenues and the concomitant ability of civil government to provide for the common good. We are certainly being affected by the greater demand on social service providers. But in an ethical sense, our lives are impacted because our brother or sister is in need and the dignity of so many lives has been diminished. When this is the context for our understanding, do we have a choice but to find a respectful way that leads to a solution?

There has been much said about the need *not* to dispense

charity in a way that leads to dependency, as some good-intentioned programs in the past may have done. This is not simply a good social principle, but one that is found in religious teaching as well. Charity must always be given in a manner that respects the individual and not simply as a vehicle to enhance the reputation of the donor. In the Jewish tradition charity actually is a legal requirement to support your fellow person when they are in need (Deut. 15:7-8). The preeminent medieval Jewish philosopher and great Torah scholar Moses Maimonides categorized in his seminal work, Mishneh Torah, eight levels of charity (or *tzedekah* or commandment) from lowest to highest in manner and intent. Although reproduced in various ways by religious and secular writers, the list of levels of giving of Maimonides may be summarized like this:

1. The most basic level of giving is when one gives begrudgingly on behalf of someone known to him, in expectation of receiving recognition and gratitude.

2. When asked to help an acquaintance, one gives less than what is needed, but does so gladly.

3. One contributes on behalf of a poor acquaintance what is needed, openheartedly, without waiting to be asked.

4. One buys something for the poor person, before being asked, and does so privately without expecting any recognition for the good deed.

5. One gives his own possession, "the shirt off his back," to someone he does not know, but who is known to the recipient.

6. One gives to someone she knows, but anonymously.

7. One gives to the poor without knowing who will receive, nor does the recipient know who gave the gift. It is a good deed, done solely from the goodness that is within us.

8. And the highest level of giving is to strengthen the person by, for example, becoming a business partner, or helping her find employment, or offering an interest-free loan that will lead to self-sufficiency.[1]

Charity is also central to the teachings of Hinduism and Buddhism as well, and as noted earlier it is also one of the Five Pillars of Islam. In the end, charity is an obligation of all our religions.

The highest form of charity is not a handout, but a loan. Extending a loan treats the recipient as a peer who participates in this transaction by the promise of repayment. The individual's dignity is respected, with no danger of subservience or dependency.

If we are to think and act anew, we must renew our belief in the foundational principle of the inherent dignity of all human life. This will require us to put back the ethical and moral elements into all aspects of human engagement. But on a more basic level, it will require us to recognize all those that we meet as our sister and brother. It will mean looking into the eyes of the poor and marginalized and seeing the image and likeness of our God and listening with reverence to their stories. It will mean acknowledging that how I choose to live my life directly impacts the lives of many who are less fortunate. It will require our churches and social structures to commit to work toward a more equitable society. It will demand that we not separate the virtue of charity from the virtue of justice. And it will mean that we never settle or compromise for any less.

Chapter 4
Charity and Justice
How We Live in Relationship to Each Other

> *The joys and the hopes, the griefs and the anxieties of the men and women of this age, especially those who are poor or in any way afflicted, these are the joys and hopes, the griefs and anxieties of the followers of Christ.*

These words that begin the Second Vatican Council's Pastoral Constitution on the Church in the Modern World (*Gaudium et Spes*), proclaimed in December 1965, inspired and energized a whole generation of Catholics to embrace a new vision of society and Church. Along with other social movements of the 1960s, it brought about a renewal not seen in the Church for five hundred years. Catholics again left behind a parochial mindset in order to become engaged in public society in a truly significant way.

When Pope Benedict XVI promulgated his first encyclical, *Deus Caritas Est* in 2006, most people were taken by surprise. This pope, who had spent a fair amount of his career defining and overseeing doctrinal orthodoxy, chose the subject of *caritas* or love for his first encyclical. In the first part of that impressive (if short by encyclical standards) document, he situates the Gospel mandate of charity within a philosophical context and explains its divine origins. The second part of the encyclical addresses very practical applications of charity on a personal and on a social level. Benedict extols the contributions of agencies like Caritas (Catholic Charities) and also challenges such organizations to be clear about what makes them distinct from other humanitarian groups.

Even though he is a theologian and not an academic schooled in organizational development, Benedict gives us a blueprint for Catholic charitable organizations. He emphasizes the need for professional development while also insisting on the need for a "formation of the heart" by charitable workers, "to be led to that encounter with God in Christ which awakens their love and opens their spirits to others" (*Deus Caritas Est*, 31). This encyclical has been well received and continues to be used as a valued document for study and formation.

His second encyclical, *Spe Salvi* (On Christian Hope, 2007), is a spiritual reflection on the impact and necessity of hope in the lives of believers. The third encyclical of Pope Benedict XVI, *Caritas in Veritate*, released in 2009, received the same amount of attention as *Deus Caritas Est* (2006) when it was first promulgated. However, since that time one would be hard-pressed to see it being actively promoted or discussed. That is one reason that this book is being written: we must not lose sight of the wisdom and teaching held within this encyclical. Its wisdom reaffirms that the virtues of charity and justice are inseparable: "Charity is at the heart of the Church's social doctrine" (*Caritas in Veritate*, 2) and "Justice is the primary way of charity" (*Deus Caritas Est*, 6).

There might, however, be another reason for the benign neglect of this encyclical. While *Deus Caritas Est* is aspirational in presenting a vision of charity in action, *Caritas in Veritate* is much more a social and practical blueprint that is specific in its demands and strategies to flesh out the virtue of justice. It is much more difficult to read *Caritas in Veritate* and remain comfortable with the lifestyle we have grown accustomed to. But no matter how hard we try to ignore their demands, charity and justice together are the two feet of discipleship.

The Bible on Charity and Justice

If we take another look back at the Hebrew Scriptures, we see that the God of Israel is a God of justice who protects and defends the poor. The prophets tell us many times over that the test of Israel's faithfulness is the treatment of the poor and vulnerable: widows, orphans, and aliens. In summarizing this point, the respected scholar Walter Brueggemann writes: "In biblical faith, the doing of justice is the primary expectation of God."[1]

Frequently readers of the prophets will relegate to these anointed spokespersons the mistaken notion that their primary mission was foretelling the future. Their role is more correctly seen as people chosen by God to relay a vision: "Thus saith the Lord God. . . ." However the vision has more to do with the present reality than with the future; more with how things should be than with how things will be. The prophet looks at the present day and sees that it does not conform to God's will, that society does not reflect the values of biblical law or tradition, that individuals have forgotten the moral order to which they should aspire. And so we find some of the most passionate and colorful passages in Scripture coming from the mouths of these determined messengers.

When Jeremiah was excoriating the unfaithful and idolatrous Israelites, he also reminded them:

> For scoundrels are found among my people;
>   they take over the goods of others. . . .
> Therefore they have become great and rich . . .
>   they do not judge with justice
> the cause of the orphan, to make it prosper,
>   and they do not defend the rights of the needy (5:26, 28).

In the famous call of Amos we see the prominence of the

virtue of justice in establishing a society acceptable to our God:

> Let justice roll down like waters
> And righteousness like an everflowing stream (5:24).

And, finally, there is Micah's equally familiar reminder that provides a summary of God's expectations for any and all disciples:

> He has told you, O mortal, what is good;
> And what does the Lord require of you
> but to do justice, and to love kindness,
> and to walk humbly with your God? (5:8)

As we begin to talk about justice there might be confusion or misunderstandings stemming from the common definitions we are accustomed to use generally and rather loosely. Aristotle identified three types of justice: legal, commutative, and distributive. *Legal* justice deals with the demands of law and concerns itself with crime and punishment. *Commutative* justice refers to rendering each person what is their due. *Distributive* justice concerns the just allocation of goods in society.

For our purposes we must talk about another kind of justice: ethical or biblical justice. This justice is based not on human reasoning or experience, but rather on the justice that marks the dealings of God within human history. We find this type of justice especially in the words of the prophets. Justice in the prophetic view deals with concrete actions, not abstractions. It refers to the hard work of transforming the unjust structures of society. The prophets offered a firm critique of what was wrong. They offered an alternative vision that we must reclaim as our own today. As the U. S. bishops wrote: "Central to the biblical presentation of justice is that the justice of a community is measured by its treatment of the powerless in society" (*Economic Justice for All*, 38).

While people sometimes look at the preaching of Jesus as revolutionary and presenting a totally new vision, in fact he stands squarely in the tradition of the Old Testament prophets. Remember that the Gospel of Luke tells us that for his first public sermon or homily, he chose a passage from the book of the prophet Isaiah: "[H]e has sent me to bring good news to the oppressed, to bind up the brokenhearted, to proclaim liberty to the captives, and release to the prisoners" (61:1-2). As Jesus further develops his teaching, he defines how inclusive and constitutive this unity of charity and justice is by using parables and actions, especially the Good Samaritan (Luke 10), the Last Judgment (Matthew 25), and the Washing of the Feet (John 13). We can profit by looking at these three passages together.

In the Parable of the Good Samaritan, after placing together the two laws—"to love God with all your heart, soul, strength, and mind" and "to love your neighbor as yourself"—in a way that they can never be separated, a lawyer asks Jesus, "And who is my neighbor?" Jesus tells the story of a man who is robbed and beaten and left to die by the side of the road. When a priest and someone trained in the law, people of his own tribe, saw this man in need, they crossed to the other side of the road and passed by. But a Samaritan—a stranger and member of a tribe with whom any contact was forbidden—came upon him and was moved with pity. He bandaged the man, took him to an inn, and paid the innkeeper to continue caring for him. Then Jesus asked the lawyer which of the men who passed by was a neighbor to the man who had been attacked. The lawyer answered, "The one who showed him mercy." And Jesus said to him, "Go and do likewise" (Luke 10:25-37). Jesus thus redefined neighbor for all generations to follow to be anyone and everyone, showing the special connection between those in need and those with the ability to help.

As I noted in chapter 1, the Parable of the Last Judgment is one of the best known and powerful teachings of Jesus. The ultimate criteria of judgment become not the keeping of ritual precepts; instead, the test of true religion will be how we respond to the hungry, the homeless, the naked—to those in need.

The Washing of the Feet is a ritual we reenact each year on Holy Thursday during the Mass of the Lord's Supper. In chapter 13 of the Gospel of John we read that Jesus took off his robe, tied a towel around his waist, poured water in a basin, and began to wash his disciples' feet. Even though they protested, Jesus insisted on demonstrating to his closest friends that we are here to serve each other. Discipleship is not predicated on power or status but on service and our ability to care for one another.

Just as Jesus connects love of God with love and service of neighbor in a way that they can never be separated, so also charity and justice can never again be pursued one without the other.

Social Justice—What Does It Mean?

The term "social justice" was first used in the mid-nineteenth century by Father Taparelli D'Azaglio, a counselor to Pope Leo XIII who wrote the first modern encyclical on social matters in response to the dehumanizing effect of industrialization. That term was first used in an encyclical in 1931 by Pope Pius XI, *Quadragesimo Anno*. This encyclical, promulgated on the fortieth anniversary of the encyclical *Rerum Novarum* of Pope Leo XIII (1891), addressed the reconstruction of the social order that was a result of the Great Depression. Social justice addresses the welfare of the greater public and how society functions. Inherent in it are the principles of the common good, subsidiarity or including people at all levels in decisions that affect them, and the preferential option for the poor.

The concept of social justice is further developed by Pope Paul VI in his encyclical *Populorum Progressio*, which he promulgated in 1967. In *Caritas in Veritate* Pope Benedict XVI draws heavily from the thought of Pope Paul VI. He emphasizes the concept of authentic human development espoused by Paul VI:

> In *development programmes*, the principle of the *centrality of the human person*, as the subject primarily responsible for development, must be preserved. The principal concern must be to improve the actual living conditions of the people in a given region, thus enabling them to carry out those duties which their poverty does not presently allow them to fulfill (*Caritas in Veritate*, 47).

When applied to individuals, this concept of authentic human development assures that they have the possibility to take ownership of their lives to the extent that they are able. It is applied to societies and economic systems in order to ensure that they guarantee that all members are engaged and allowed to participate in decisions that affect their lives. The first goal of all social and political structures should be the enhancement of human life: "The theme of development can be identified with the inclusion-in-relation of all individuals and peoples within the one community of the human family . . ." (*Caritas in Veritate*, 54).

Again Pope Benedict reminds us of the danger of compartmentalizing the human experience by separating the economic sphere from the social. "*The whole Church, in all her being and acting—when she proclaims, when she celebrates, when she performs works of charity—is engaged in promoting integral human development . . . [A]uthentic human development concerns the whole of the person in every single dimension"* (*Caritas in Veritate*, 11). The Holy Father also wrote: "The risk for our time is that the *de facto* interdependence of people and nations is not matched by ethical interaction of consciences and minds that would give rise to truly human development" (*Caritas in Veritate*, 9).

Foundational to the teachings of the Scriptures is the belief that we are called upon to live in community. This community is premised on the relationship human beings have to one another. We are neighbors, but we are more. We are sisters and brothers called to value and practice the virtues of charity and justice. This is of ultimate importance in how we act as citizens and neighbors in the United States, and it should define what is expected of us in serving the least of those who are members of our national family.

There are many ways that we as individuals can practice charity and justice and service in our daily lives. Some people, such as those who work in Catholic Charities agencies, dedicate their lives to serving others full time, but there are others who have found ways to use their own special talents to serve their neighbors.

In Washington, D.C., a young chef who cooked in acclaimed restaurants quit the restaurant business to spend more time with his family. Instead of working in restaurants serving those who can afford to eat out, he decided to put his skills to work running a soup kitchen. For the past nine years Steve Badt has run the kitchen operations at Miriam's Kitchen in Washington, D.C. Miriam's Kitchen provides free, homemade meals that sometimes include omelettes, grits, and strawberry shortcake, and other support services to more than four thousand homeless men and women each year. In a profile, Badt said that the realization hit him that "once you're on the street, it's hard to get back on your feet." He decided to dedicate his training to serve others, thinking, "if I can start these guys off with a beautiful meal and a great meal and a nutritious meal, that [might] increase the odds that maybe they'll get housing, that maybe they'll get off drugs, that maybe they'll have a good day."[2]

Forty-year-old celebrity chef José Andrés runs top restaurants in Washington, D.C. and Beverly Hills, where he offers avant garde taste experiences to rich and powerful diners. But he also shares his talent in a different way—he volunteers at Washington's Central Kitchen (DCCK), founded on the premise that "when fighting poverty, one must fight to win by using every resource available" and not wasting potential, "whether food, money, or people." This community kitchen recycles more than a ton of surplus food each day and turns it into 4,500 meals that are distributed throughout the greater Washington, D.C., region. For seventeen years Chef Andrés, who calls himself "a pilgrim from Spain," has been peeling potatoes and lending his expertise to the kitchen workers, who are also students in DCCK's Culinary Job Training program. These men and women, many of whom had been homeless or imprisoned, are equipped with professional and life skills and opportunities that enable them to move on to real jobs in restaurant kitchens in the area. Chef Andrés has hired ten of DCCK's graduates and personally has mentored fifty interns. He also has helped raise $1.5 million for the organization's programs. He expressed his philosophy in an interview on "60 Minutes": "Chefs of America, we should be more outspoken about the way we are feeding America," not only in the great restaurants of America that are frequented by only about 3 percent of Americans, but "we should be more committed about the other 97 percent of Americans who do not come to our restaurants."[3]

There are tens of thousands of examples like these across America—men, women, and children who are committed to serving those who are struggling, from the mentally ill homeless person sleeping on the street to the family down the block having trouble paying their bills. Each of us has a talent or a treasure we can share. Our goal should be to multiply those thousands to millions.

Ultimately, the way we treat each other and care for each other—from the individual helping hand to how our leaders work on our behalf—will determine what our society and our world will be like. We must see each other as family, because we are all brothers and sisters in Christ, children of a loving God.

Chapter 5
The Common Good and Free Markets
In Service to Humanity

> What is needed . . . is a market that permits the free operation, in conditions of equal opportunity, of enterprises in pursuit of different institutional ends. Alongside profit-oriented private enterprise, and the various types of public enterprise, there must be room for commercial entities based on mutualist principles and pursuing social ends to take root and express themselves (Caritas in Veritate, 38).

A man was going on a journey so he commissioned his servants to take care of his property while he was gone. To the first, he gave five talents (metal weights used as money), to another servant he gave two, and to yet another, one talent, each according to his ability. Then he went away. The one who had received five talents went off and traded with them and made five more. The one who had the two talents made two more. But the servant who had received the one talent went off and dug a hole in the ground and hid his master's money, because he was afraid. When their master returned, he was very pleased with the two servants who had doubled their investments and put them in charge of many things. But the man was angry with the one who had hidden his talent, calling him wicked and lazy, and saying that he "ought to have invested my money with the bankers" so that he at least would have received interest when he returned (Matt. 25: 14-27).

Jesus liked to speak to the multitudes in parables, and the one recounted above seems to fit our situation today, although I'm not sure he would have been pleased with the results of his investment with the bankers. But what this reading from Scripture can tell us on closer inspection is that we have been entrusted with our Master's estate and that it is incumbent upon us to use our God-given talents—the treasure of our personal realm— to build his presence on earth. Or else. That may not seem consistent with the idea of Christian kindness, but it does maintain the analogy that God's dealings with humankind are not merely benevolent, but are wise and just in their recognition of moral effort.[1]

In *Caritas in Veritate*, Pope Benedict XVI observes that our tendency in modern society to a consumerist and utilitarian view of life results in "serious errors in the areas of education, politics, social action, and morals," which includes the economy, which "has been included for some time now" (*Caritas in Veritate*, 34). Based on our belief that we are in charge of our own lives and the society we create, we are convinced that the economy, too, "must be autonomous, that it must be shielded from 'influences' of a moral character" (34).

But as Benedict notes, these beliefs have led us to "abuse the economic process in a thoroughly destructive way. In the long term, these convictions have led to economic, social and political systems that trample upon personal and social freedom, and are therefore unable to deliver the justice that they promise" (34).

All of us have been given gifts from God—love and truth among them. Some of us are talented at finance, others at making and selling goods, or providing the services needed for a society to operate. We must not, however, forget *why* we've been given these gifts, and that is to further God's work on earth by creating and sustaining economic, social, and political frameworks that ensure that each person is afforded the opportunity to develop fully their own lives according to the gifts they have received. This includes those who are poor.

How does this work in a market economy?

First, the market must not be the place where the strong subdue the weak (recall the words of the prophet Jeremiah about the "scoundrels taking over the goods of others"). Economics and finance are not of themselves dangerous instruments, but they can become so when they are used for purely selfish ends. Society should not have to protect itself from the market, since the market can become lethal when ideologies and cultures emerge that embrace the "greed is good" mantra.

Second, we recognize that the market is an effective tool—and can even be a beneficial one—for the exchange of goods and services that give us what we need and want. The market economy of the United States has enabled an era of innovation and development unprecedented in the history of humankind. But it is also subject to *distributive justice* and *social justice* (*Caritas in Veritate*, 35), because there is a broader social and political context in which it operates.

Third, "*every economic decision has a moral consequence*" (*Caritas in Veritate*, 37). In the global economy in which we now live, we cannot rely on a simplistic formula that allows economic activity to be free-wheeling and relies on government and political structures alone to assure that the wealth created is equitably distributed. In a year that has seen banks fail, mortgages foreclosed, and huge corporations that pay no U.S. taxes, it is clear to us that a new way of thinking and acting in our economic sphere is needed.

Finally, in the words of Pope Benedict XVI: "*The economy needs ethics in order to function correctly*—not any ethics whatsoever, but an ethics which is people-centered" (*Caritas in Veritate*, 45).

Our current binary system of market plus state creates an environment that is adversarial instead of collaborative, and it is far from focused on the common good. The New York Stock Exchange and NASDAQ were created out of the sheer imaginative power of American business people. Our form of government was created from the sheer genius of a few hearty colonialists who had an enlightened vision for society. Thomas Edison saw the potential in telegraphic technology, which gave birth to the General Electric Corporation, which still embraces innovation, as evidenced in its corporate identity slogan, "imagination at work." It is time for us to embrace that same spirit of innovation to create new forms of business that are measured and rewarded by how they enhance the lives of Americans at the bottom of economic and social life as well as those at the top.

Finance as an Instrument of Development

Benedict does believe that the financial services industry can play a key role in his new vision for society, but that it needs to be re-imagined: "*Finance*, therefore—through the renewed structures and operating methods that have to be designed after its misuse, which wreaked such havoc on the real economy—now needs to go back to being an *instrument directed towards improved wealth creation and development*. Insofar as they are instruments, the entire economy and finance, not just certain sectors, must be used in an ethical way so as to create suitable conditions for human development and for the development of peoples" (*Caritas in Veritate*, 65).

In the mid-1970s, Professor Muhammad Yunus set out to resolve the problem of rural poverty in Bangladesh by making sure "that the credit system serves the poor, and not vice-versa," and founded what became the Grameen Bank, which provides credit without requiring any collateral to the poorest of the poor in rural Bangladesh. His goal was to reverse the vicious cycle of "low income, low saving and low investment," into a virtuous circle of "low income, injection of credit, investment, more income, more savings, more investment, more income."[2]

Professor Yunus believed that poor people are the same everywhere, and that you can always trust them to pay back what they have borrowed. It is the concept of trust in poor people that has made Grameen programs successful with its borrowers worldwide. According to its website, as of April 2010, Grameen Bank has 8.1 million borrowers, 97 percent of whom are women.[3] With 2,564 branches, Grameen Bank provides services in more than 81,000 villages. The bank is owned by the rural poor whom it serves, and in Bangladesh, borrowers own 90 percent of its shares, while the remaining 10 percent is owned by the government. And as Professor Yunus is quick to point out, the Grameen Bank has had this success while also becoming a profitable enterprise.

In 2006, Professor Yunus and Grameen Bank received the Nobel Peace Prize for "their efforts to create economic and social development from below," as the Nobel citation reads. In 2009 Yunus was awarded the Presidential Medal of Freedom by President Barack Obama for his pioneering efforts to lift people out of poverty.[4]

In 2008 Professor Yunus brought his idea to the United States. Grameen America launched its first branch in Jackson Heights, Queens, in January 2008, and in Manhattan in May 2010. Grameen America follows the group-lending model established in Bangladesh, where groups of five people who receive a Grameen micro-loan learn financial literacy, start savings accounts, and borrow money as a unit. Each individual develops a plan to start a small business, and the group decides who gets the first loan. If any one borrower is ever late in repaying a loan, loans to everyone in the group are suspended. So far the bank has been successful in transferring its model to the United States. It has provided more than $6 million to 2,800 borrowers, mainly women, living below the U.S. poverty line. Grameen America currently maintains a repayment rate of over 99 percent.[5]

The Method of Action of Grameen Bank

1. Start with the problem rather than the solution: a credit system must be based on a survey of the social background rather than on a pre-established banking technique.

2. Adopt a progressive attitude: development is a long-term process which depends on the aspirations and commitment of the economic operators.

3. Make sure that the credit system serves the poor, and not vice-versa: credit officers visit the villages, enabling them to get to know the borrowers.

4. Establish priorities for action vis-à-vis the target population: serve the most poverty-stricken people needing investment resources, who have no access to credit.

5. At the beginning, restrict credit to income-generating production operations, freely selected by the borrower. Make it possible for the borrower to be able to repay the loan.

6. Lean on solidarity groups: small informal groups consisting of co-opted members coming from the same background and trusting each other.

7. Associate savings with credit without it being necessarily a prerequisite.

8. Combine close monitoring of borrowers with procedures which are simple and as standardized as possible.

9. Do everything possible to ensure the system's financial balance.

10. Invest in human resources: training leaders will provide them with real development ethics based on rigor, creativity, understanding and respect for the rural environment.[6]

In *Caritas in Veritate*, Pope Benedict also is concerned with the stability of large enterprises, noting that frequent turnover at the top undermines the executive's commitment to the long-term health of the organization and can lead to abandoning responsibility toward its stakeholders, including employees, suppliers, customers, consumers, the environment, and the broader society in favor of shareholders, who may not have any ties to the communities in which the company operates or does business.

The worldwide success of the corporate social responsibility movement parallels the Church's conviction that "*business management cannot concern itself only with the interests of the proprietors but must also assume responsibility for all the other stakeholders who contribute to the life of the business*" (*Caritas in Veritate*, 40).

Fortunes at the Bottom of the Pyramid

> *These unhappy times call for the building of plans that rest upon the forgotten, the unorganized but the indispensable units of economic power . . . that build from the bottom up and not from the top down, that put their faith once more in the forgotten man at the bottom of the economic pyramid.*[7]

These words by Franklin D. Roosevelt in his April 7, 1932, radio address, "The Forgotten Man," are echoed in *Caritas in Veritate*, as Pope Benedict advises us to see those less fortunate in a new way: "the poor are not to be considered a 'burden', but a resource, even from the purely economic point of view" (*Caritas in Veritate*, 35).

Grameen Bank is one example of this "bottom of the economic pyramid" concept introduced by Roosevelt and more recently explored and celebrated by Professors C. K. Prahalad and Stuart L. Hart. This idea acknowledges that these traditionally overlooked and unserved people at the bottom have considerable combined purchasing power. Their theory proposes that if companies are innovative enough to create or tailor their products to the economic realities and life needs of the poor, a significant profit can be made and, at the same time, the entry of businesses into the market has the potential to improve the quality of life of its customers.

Others view the poor as producers whose products or services are bought by other poor. As Aneel Karnani, Associate Professor of Strategy at the University of Michigan's Ross School of Business, observes: to increase the income of the poor, we need to create employment opportunities for the poor.[8] In either case, the bottom of the pyramid model can bring about impressive social change.

One strong example of such a pyramid model is CEMEX and Patrimonio Hoy in Mexico. Mexico faces a severe housing shortage that affects the daily lives of more than twenty million people. CEMEX, a Mexican-based, global building-solutions company, conducted a research project in 1998 to determine whether it was possible to design products that would contribute significantly to a better quality of life for low-income communities. CEMEX learned that the minimal buying power of this population resulted in a low level of service, a lack of ability to obtain the requisite financial resources, a lack of knowledge of the building process, and a lack of access to technical support, all leading to a construction process that did not work. In response to these findings, CEMEX created Patrimonio Hoy, a progressive housing program that serves the people in low-income communities.

Through the program, packages of materials are ordered

in the sequence in which they can be used, thereby solving the problem of storing excess materials that would come with a traditional order, as well as allowing the buyers to pay in allotments as they have the money. The packages are purchased through a CEMEX-funded micro-financing program. When the buyers have saved 20 percent of the price of the materials needed for completing the construction project, credit is granted for the remaining 80 percent. In 2008 the weekly charge per family was about $16.50, $14 of which paid for materials, and the remaining $2.50 covered services, including free access to technical consultants, fixed prices guaranteed for seventy weeks, one year of materials storage, and home delivery of materials.

In an article written for Chamberpost.com, Israel Moreno Barceló, founder and general manager of Patrimonio Hoy for CEMEX in Mexico, described how the program creates a collaborative network within the community consisting of families in need of better housing conditions, CEMEX distributors, and CEMEX financial services and technical advice, including an architect who helps design homes to optimize space and reduce waste.

As of May 2008, a total of 205,000 Mexican families had benefited through Patrimonio Hoy, and $94 million in loans had been granted, with an on-time payment rate of more than 99 percent. The program has also been successfully implemented in Colombia, Venezuela, Nicaragua, and Costa Rica. Ideally CEMEX would like to replicate Patrimonio Hoy in other markets where the company operates and where the socio-economic conditions make it financially viable.[9]

The challenge for America is to take the experiences of companies like Grameen and CEMEX and create new models that can provide market-based opportunities for those at the bottom of our economic pyramids.

Hybrids —New Models of Business Enterprise

The very plurality of institutional forms of business gives rise to a market which is not only more civilized but also more competitive (Caritas in Veritate, 46).

In the United States the "business" of taking care of the poor and other social welfare concerns has evolved into a non-profit sector that is legally and practically set apart from for-profit companies. But, as Pope Benedict observes, "the traditionally valid distinction between profit-based companies and non-profit organizations can no longer do full justice to reality, or offer practical direction for the future" (*Caritas in Veritate*, 46). Fortunately, new hybrid models of business have emerged in recent years. One comment posted on our on-line forum suggested expanding the presence of "B" corporations. Another noted the company of TOMS Shoes and its idea of "One for One." Another hybrid, the Catholic-based Economy of Communion, has had some success in Europe and is growing, although more slowly, in North America.

TOMS Shoes and One for One

In 2006 Blake Mycoskie was traveling in Argentina when he noticed that many children had no shoes to protect their feet. Wanting to help, he created TOMS Shoes, a company that would match every pair of shoes purchased with a pair of new shoes given to a child in need. Blake returned to Argentina with a group of family, friends, and staff later that year with 10,000 pairs of shoes made possible by TOMS customers. To date, TOMS has given over 600,000 pairs of shoes to children in need around the world.[10]

The TOMS One for One business model transforms customers into benefactors, supplying the capital that allows growth and a profit for a truly sustainable business with a social mission. This one-for-one idea is spreading. Ralph Lauren's co-branded Polo Rugby TOMS donates a pair of shoes for every pair sold, and Element Skateboards has issued limited edition TOMS + Element shoes as well as a one-for-one skateboard program: with every skateboard purchased, one is given to a child at the Indigo Skate Camp in Durban, South Africa.

TOMS is proof that business and philanthropy don't have to be mutually exclusive. And the company, as noted in a profile on *The Wall Street Journal* goes "a step further than most in blurring the difference between brand and charity; the brand doesn't exist outside the charitable work. Its success shows that good works can be a powerful profit engine."[11]

Economy of Communion

An article in the November 30, 2009 issue of *America* magazine reported that

it is rare for a specific project to be given a favourable mention in a papal encyclical, but *Caritas in Veritate* seems to present an exception. When Pope Benedict XVI described the "broad intermediate area" between non-profit and for-profit sectors with the buzz-phrase "economy of communion," some connected the dots with the Focolare movement's network of businesses in which profit serves as "a means for achieving human and social ends."[12]

Like the thinking that led to the establishment of micro-financing and micro-enterprises, the Focolare-inspired Economy of Communion (EOC) represents "a new way of ordering business and economic life"—a model based upon sustainable growth that contributes to the common good. EOC businesses commit a share of their profits to (1) support the development of people and communities in need, (2) advocate for a "culture of giving" to replace our "culture of having," and (3) grow their businesses in order to create jobs and wealth. More than 750 businesses are involved in EOC in various ways. There are 413 businesses in Europe and 35 in North America.[13]

The EOC concept is attracting interest in academic circles. On Saturday, April 24, 2010, Seton Hall University in South Orange, New Jersey, featured an all-day forum on Catholic social justice. Much of the afternoon was devoted to discussing Economy of Communion.[14]

Sofia Violins and the Economy of Communion

Musicians around the world are familiar with the high quality and value pricing of Sofia Violins string instruments. Each Sofia instrument is individually handcrafted by expert violin makers, many of whom have international reputations. While Sofia depends on the expertise of its luthiers, seventy-year-old Sofia Violins' CEO John Welch believes people are the most important part of any business.

Welch is devoted to the Economy of Communion because of the positive experience he has had using its model. Sofia Violins, which is based in Indiana, produces about 350 handmade violins a year. Many of them are crafted by luthiers in Eastern Europe and has provided citizens from these emerging markets with a valuable skill.

Welch acknowledges that it can be a challenge to assist others and also ensure the financial stability of the business. Yet he says that helping others has always proved rewarding and agrees with his beliefs about responsible business practices. He believes it is good business "to live God in the present moment."[15]

B Corporations

B corporations (the B stands for Benefit) are companies that work to solve social and environmental problems in addition to earning returns for shareholders. By adhering to a "triple-bottom line"—they are required to create a material positive impact on society and the environment while they provide shareholder returns and maintain higher standards of accountability and transparency—B corporations are an alternative to the short-term focus of public companies that are pressured to generate quick returns for shareholders. To become a "certified B," a company must meet rigorous standards and rewrite its mission statement to reflect the values of the B corporation community. The companies are certified by the nonprofit organization, B Lab. There are now more than three hundred certified B corporations. A rating system for evaluating triple-bottom line companies, called the Global Impact Investing Rating System (GIIRS), provides a way to compare and contrast the environmental and social performance of companies looking for investment capital. These ratings can be used to encourage significant institutional investment in entrepreneurial social enterprises.[16]

Benefit corporations are demonstrating that business and social change can work together.

Evergreen Lodge, a historic tourist lodge just outside of Yosemite National Park, hires at-risk young people from low-income areas and teaches them hospitality industry skills.[17] In 2001 the owners formed a limited liability corporation (LLC) and raised $15 million in debt and equity from socially minded investors and nonprofits. Since then Evergreen has expanded from eighteen to ninety cabins, increased revenue from $500,000 in 2001 to $5 million (2008)[18], and helped more than sixty young adults get their lives back on track.

Another example of a B corporation is Greyston Bakery in

Yonkers, New York, a $6.5 million for-profit business that is a model for social enterprise. The company has built a coalition of employees, people from the community, and shareholders, and hires men and women who have little or no credentialed work experience, many of whom have backgrounds that include homelessness, incarceration, substance abuse, welfare dependence, domestic violence, and illiteracy. Greyston Bakery produces brownies, cakes, and tarts, including brownies for Ben & Jerry's line of ice cream. Their Do-Goodie Brownie was featured in Oprah Winfrey's O Magazine. Greyston Bakery, through its profit generation, is a substantial source of revenue for programs of the Greyston Foundation, which offers affordable childcare in the community, affordable housing for homeless and low-income families, and affordable health care for persons with HIV.[19]

B corporations may be certified, but they are not yet recognized as a legal entity in most of the country. In April 2010, however, Maryland became the first state to pass and sign into law Benefit Corporation legislation. Now certified B companies in Maryland will legally be able to consider the interests of employees, the environment, and the larger community in their decision-making—and directors can't be sued if they take actions deemed to be damaging to shareholder financial interests. Vermont followed in May with its own Benefit Corporation legislation.

All of these innovative business models formed around a social mission offer new means of achieving economic and social justice while they turn a profit. And they will strengthen our nation by putting first what is most important: the well-being of all people, especially the least among us.

Chapter 6
A Nation That Cares for Everyone
What We Ask of Our Government

> *I would like to remind everyone, especially governments engaged in boosting the world's economic and social assets, that the primary capital to be safeguarded and valued is man, the human person in his or her integrity: "Man is the source, the focus and the aim of all economic and social life"* (Benedict XVI, *Caritas in Veritate*, 25).

The conversation that has been taking place in our country since the near total collapse of Wall Street in 2008 has been discussed in terms of institutions and groups: the government, banks, Main Street, Wall Street, the jobless, the uninsured.

What we seem to forget is that behind each of these inscrutable walls are people, human beings, individual persons whose lives have been torn apart, sometimes by their own decisions, more often because of the decisions of others.

Every day Catholic Charities workers encounter men, women, and children who are hungry, homeless, sick, or in need in some basic way. And each of them has a unique story.

As we grapple with the concept of poverty in America, we must reach beyond the statistics, surveys, and documents that comprise our official response to the poor. We owe it to these people, who are our brothers and sisters in Christ, to treat them as more than nameless and faceless numbers. Doing so makes it far too easy to set them aside into some category that we can designate as "the other." After all, Jesus did not ask us to simply think about caring for our neighbor. He gave us the Great Commandment: "Love your neighbor" (Luke 10:27). It was—and still is—a call to action. It is a call to community.

When we think of poverty, our initial thinking may be that it is a problem for the government to solve. What we forget is that we the people are the government, and our government is itself grounded in the call to charity in truth. So I propose that we think and act anew about what it means, as our Founding Fathers suggested, to hold certain truths to be self-evident. Let's affirm and act on the truth that all men and women are created equal.

As a people we have tried to create institutions and to take political actions that reflect God's love and truth in society.

In response to the Great Depression that followed the market crash of 1929, the United States Congress enacted and President Franklin Roosevelt signed into law the Social Security Act. The preamble to this original 1935 Act stated that it was "to provide for the general welfare by establishing a system of Federal old-age benefits, and by enabling the several States to make more adequate provision for aged persons, blind persons, dependent and crippled children, maternal and child welfare, public health. . . ."[1] And certainly since that time, social security has protected tens of millions from poverty in retirement and in other ways.

In the 1960s, when half of the people over sixty-five had no health insurance, descendents of former slaves had little voice in our electoral system, and only a third of American children were receiving early childhood education, we took another step toward promoting the general welfare by declaring the War on Poverty through legislation introduced by President Lyndon Johnson. By putting into place measures ranging from Medicare to Head Start, student loans, and civil rights, we made a commitment to be not only a rich and powerful society, but a Great

Society. Under President Nixon the United States adopted the earned income tax credit, which has helped tens of millions of the lowest-paid working Americans come closer to self-sufficiency. The welfare safety net was again revised in the 1990s.

Although each of these steps was quite controversial in its time, together they greatly contributed to reducing poverty. In fact, the poverty rate dropped from 22 percent in 1958 to 11 percent in 1973, climbed again in the 1980s, and then dropped from 15.1 percent in 1993 to 11.8 percent in 1999.[2] But the number of poor remains enormous, and is certainly disproportionate to and out of line with such a wealthy society as ours.

In *Caritas in Veritate*, Benedict XVI advises us that as we

take to heart the lessons of the current economic crisis, which sees the State's *public authorities* directly involved in correcting errors and malfunctions, it seems more realistic to *re-evaluate their role* and their powers, which need to be prudently reviewed and remodeled so as to enable them, perhaps through new forms of engagement, to address the challenges of today's world (24).

So, how in the twenty-first century do we re-evaluate the role and powers of governments and remodel them to help us leave fewer behind?

First, we need to think anew about poverty.

For those who are not enmeshed in poverty issues on a daily basis, a slight detour to provide some history may be helpful.

In 1963, in connection with the War on Poverty, Mollie Orshansky, an economist and statistician at the Social Security Administration, developed an official measure of poverty for use by the U.S. government that was based on a low-cost food plan— one determined to be suitable for emergencies when funds were low. Orshansky knew from a 1955 survey on household food consumption, the most recent data available then, that "families of three or more persons spent about one third of their after-tax income on food." Using this information, she "then multiplied the cost of the USDA economy food plan by three to arrive at the minimal yearly income a family would need." According to her calculations, a family of four "would spend $1,033 for food per year. Using her formula based on the 1955 survey, she arrived at $3,100 a year ($1,033 x 3) as the poverty threshold for a family of four in 1963."[3] In 1969 a method of adjusting this scale based on the Consumer Price Index was adopted to designate the poverty thresholds and became the federal government's official statistical definition for poverty, a life of severe deprivation and economic hardship.

Essentially, the same 45-year-old formula—based on 1955 data—is still used today to calculate poverty.

However, the world and the poor have changed substantially since then. This measure is less and less useful, because the cost of food has dropped in relation to other components of the cost of living, and even many working Americans do not make enough to cover their basic living expenses.

In the fall of 2008, Catholic Charities USA began conducting a quarterly snapshot survey of our member agencies to track how the economic recession was changing the face of the poor in our country. The results, which are posted on our website, offer a dramatic account of how deeply our society is experiencing the challenges of this recession. This first-hand data reveals a nationwide increase for life-sustaining emergency services across the country. Specifically, the survey shows that these are unemployed parents; or two-income families struggling to make ends meet; or pregnant women and teens, homeless with nowhere to turn; or even former donors to Catholic Charities organizations now in need of help; and also repeat clients with deeper needs and greater barriers to self-sufficiency. In other words, we are seeing new and underserved populations continuing to request help in sobering numbers; people who never imagined that they would not have solid and steady employment or be able to provide for their families in a comfortable or even adequate manner. All of this gives even more importance to a measure of poverty that accurately reflects the struggles of our fellow citizens.

A New Measure of Poverty

Several alternative measures of poverty have been proposed in the last decade. Most analyses of these measures find that an updated poverty measure would increase the percentage of those classified as poor. It is not surprising that elected officials are reluctant to redefine poverty thresholds. After all, no president or governor wants the official poverty numbers revised upward during his or her administration.

But based on the extensive experience of Catholic Charities over the past year—having added more than a million people to the number we serve—we insist that it is time to deal with this issue. In a report that made the rounds of the Group of 20 Summit in Pittsburgh in 2009, Professors Joseph E. Stiglitz and Amartya Sen wrote: "The time is ripe to shift the emphasis from measuring economic production to measuring people's well-being."[4]

We agree. By changing our focus from a body of statistics to the human person, we will be able to develop the right solutions. In the words of *Gaudium et Spes*, restated by Pope Benedict, "*Man is the source, the focus and the aim of all economic and social life*" (*Caritas in Veritate*, 25). We would do well as Catholics and people of faith to heed his words.

One new tool that Catholic Charities USA is using is

among the innovative approaches being developed today. The American Human Development Index (see the website www. MeasureofAmerica.org) is based on three indicators:

+ a long and healthy life, measured by life expectancy;
+ access to knowledge, measured by educational attainment and school enrollment; and
+ a decent standard of living, measured by median earnings.

The result is three separate measures: a health index, an education index, and an income index. After taking into account the lenses of geography, race, and gender, the three are added together and then divided by three to give the American Human Development Index.

A strength of the Human Development Index is that it can be applied geographically, and can be broken down to local congressional districts.

This approach promotes a more informed, reasoned debate using objective facts and comparisons. The information it provides empowers people to hold elected officials accountable and it connects research to action on human well-being in real, measurable twenty-first century terms.

Another more local approach has been created by the Crittenton Women's Union in Boston, Massachusetts. The Union has determined that "the real cost of living for a single mother with a toddler in Boston is $48,706, more than three times the poverty threshold"[5]—and this assumes that the family does not eat any meals out, cannot put any money into savings, and cannot afford a car. But even with working full time at minimum wage, the average single mother "still lives almost $2,000 below the federal poverty level—and that threshold is already artificially low because it encompasses Alabama and Oklahoma and other states with a low cost of living."[6] If the family receives public support through services such as food stamps or day-care it is better able to manage. But many poor working families eventually pass the official poverty line and then lose the assistance they need in order to work, such as child-care subsidies and health care.

Having real measures of the struggles facing millions of Americans, like having real marketing data for a successful business, is the first step in building a foundation for twenty-first century government solutions to poverty.

Not All Poor People Are Equal

It is easy to think of the poor as a homogenous, monolithic bloc with an unending thirst for public assistance. Nothing could be further from the truth. But that's how our government is structured to address poverty and thus the way government defines poverty.

We must not forget that these are individual human beings, each with hopes and dreams. They can, however, be grouped into several categories defined by their life experience, rather than solely by their economic status.

+ People who need help but lack the skills and abilities necessary to succeed in the work world—possibly because of a lack of education, experience, and cultural and social skills. These are often the intergenerational poor.

+ People who need help but have a limited ability to care for themselves because they are sick or have physical or mental limitations that make it difficult or impossible to provide for their basic needs. Children and the elderly are likely to fall into this category.

More on Redefining Poverty

A discussion on the "Big Idea" forum of Catholic Charities suggests that we focus on human development and redefine poverty based on regional cost of living standards. This idea calls for passing legislation and adopting regulations in each state to develop a measure based on the cost of living in metropolitan regions and what it takes to make ends meet with housing, transportation, health care, child care, education, and food. Because there is such resistance to replacing the federal measure of poverty, each department identified above could report its data using these new regional or statewide standards, which would result in a more accurate picture of poverty for that specific geographic area. This could be done in addition to reporting with the federal measure.

The Insight Center for Community Economic Development, a California-based research organization, developed the Self-Sufficiency Standard to calculate the minimum amount of income required to pay for basic needs in each county of California. It is being used as a tool to help families move from poverty to economic self-sufficiency. The standard is being used in California as a counseling/educational tool, as a benchmarking/evaluation tool, as a policymaking tool, as a planning tool, as a persuasive tool, and as a data/research tool.[7]

At the federal level, the appropriate departments (Health and Human Services, Education, Labor, Commerce, Justice, Agriculture, and HUD, for example) should adopt regulations doing the same thing on a national level. The awareness of the reality of the breadth of poverty is a first step to creating the political will for change. Benefits don't change at this step, just the acknowledgment that the benefits are far below what it takes to make ends meet.

"[The poverty line] could actually be centered on the calculated living wage. Anyone not making the living wage would be below the poverty line."[8]

✦ People with skills and experience but who still need help, possibly because they are limited by their circumstances, such as the current economic downturn with its foreclosures and millions of lost jobs. This could include the many thousands of underemployed working well below their skill levels.

Our current approach in providing aid is to take one aspect of the needs of a poor person—one deficit or disability—and supply a program to meet that specific need: food stamps for the hungry, disability income for the disabled, unemployment benefits and job training for those out of work.

This approach suffers from at least three fundamental defects. First, it fails to treat the person as a person—as a human who deserves to be heard, treated with dignity and respect, and offered help, but also as a person with the ability to decide how to live his or her own life successfully. Second, it treats a person in pieces as someone who is hungry, or needs housing, or needs help with utility bills or transportation. Third, it treats people in terms of their deficits, disabilities, and disorders, often without identifying, celebrating, and building on their strengths of character and will, as well as their assets of experience, family, and friends.

What is needed is a holistic approach, an approach well known to those on the front lines of Catholic Charities who can testify to the enormous power of listening to a person and responding to what he or she says about their particular situation.

With today's technologies, surely we can have individualized poverty prevention plans, with services tailored to the individual.

We also must be able to develop a software platform that allows sustained individualized case management, connecting available programs and resources to all of an individual's needs and challenges and drawing on all of her or his strengths and assets. We can develop a system with a single point-of-entry and personalized mentorship.

To do this we will likely need to reconfigure a lot of one-size-fits-all national rules and let local governments, local councils, and public and private partnerships pool and leverage resources and share accountability.

There are innovations taking place at state and local levels that can serve as models for a new federal approach. For example, the Iowa Successful Families Caucus works to change the way Iowa legislators think about poverty, moving the discussion beyond the traditional human services committee work to generate and coordinate solutions across all committees in the Iowa General Assembly. The Caucus successfully worked to raise the minimum wage from $5.15 to $6.20 in April of 2007 and to $7.25 in January of 2008. The group also secured funding for child-care assistance, with income eligibility set at 145 percent of the federal poverty level. In 2007, 20,448 children per month received child-care assistance in Iowa.[9]

Colorado has established the bipartisan Common Good Caucus, which brings together legislators interested in addressing poverty through public policy and private-sector efforts. In 2007 the Caucus held town hall meetings throughout the state to hear people's stories about their struggles with poverty and to engage legislators in helping find solutions. As a result, the governor's office presented an anti-poverty budget request that included a $213.5 million increase in programs aimed at fighting poverty.

In 2004, Connecticut became the first state in the nation to enact a law setting an anti-poverty target—to cut child poverty in half by 2014.

Of course, the states look to the national government for leadership, and at the federal level efforts have been ongoing since the landmark social security legislation of the 1930s. In 1996 President Bill Clinton made good on his campaign promise to "end poverty as we know it" when Congress passed the Personal Responsibility and Work Opportunity Reconciliation Act (PRWORA). The bill replaced direct financial aid to families with temporary assistance for needy families (TANF), which includes as part of the aims of the program the promotion of work, responsibility, and self-sufficiency.

Work and the ability to find work have been at the center of most government anti-poverty programs since the Social Security Act of 1935 created unemployment insurance. A common refrain from politicians is "the fastest way out of poverty is a job with a living wage." But, as we know, a person must have the skills and physical ability to work, *and* there must be work available.

Most jobs in the United States are in the private sector. However, from January 2008 through May 2010, millions of private sector jobs were lost, and unemployment as of this writing is just shy of 10 percent with over 15 million Americans seeking work. The devastation this creates is real. Again, Pope Benedict speaks to this:

> In comparison with the casualties of industrial society in the past, unemployment today provokes new forms of economic marginalization, and the current crisis can only make this situation worse. Being out of work or dependent on public or private assistance for a prolonged period undermines the freedom and creativity of the person and his family and social relationships, causing great psychological and spiritual suffering (*Caritas in Veritate*, 25).

Unemployment insurance benefits are essential, as is illustrated by the need for repeated extensions of those benefits in the current recession. But in today's rapidly changing economy and deep recession, those programs need to be rethought.

As the country's industrial landscape continues to change with a rapidity rarely seen in the past, millions of Americans are likely to need re-education and job training at multiple times throughout their working lives. If, as is true in many cases, the need for manual labor and assembly-line jobs has declined, there has been little evidence of a concomitant increase in replacement jobs for those people.

New jobs are needed, but where will they come from? We need to determine the appropriate role and relationship of the private sector and the government in fostering the innovation needed to encourage pilot programs and new approaches, to screen ideas, to invest as a catalyst, to conduct rigorous evaluation and measurement, and to identify and scale up what works.

Government must also use its authority to set the rules for financial markets and to manage the marketplace so that it serves the common good and does not cause harm and suffering.

The specifics of the recent financial crisis led to sweeping financial regulatory reform bills now (as of this writing) being reconciled by the Senate and the House. I am not qualified to judge whether this legislation correctly diagnoses what went wrong, but we can only hope that the final bill will set the nation on a more secure and healthier path.

I urge us to take seriously Pope Benedict's point about the connection between the economy and ethics: "*The economy needs ethics in order to function correctly* . . . not any ethics whatsoever, but an ethics which is people-centered" (*Caritas in Veritate*, 45). The point is that we need an excellent and effective institutional or political path of charity in the form of sound government rules designed for the common good.

The financial crisis illustrates the need to take this point seriously, but the point is much broader than the financial crisis and financial markets. We need to take this opportunity to decide if there are other reforms in the rules of market capitalism that will better serve the common good.

Benedict XVI asks us to explore new types of enterprises besides the private, public, and voluntary sectors that currently comprise the American landscape—enterprises that might embrace both public and political spheres—to enable us to strengthen this important relationship between business and ethics (*Caritas in Veritate,* 46).

As Americans we should have great confidence when we take up Pope Benedict's challenge to structure new enterprises that view profit as a means of achieving a more humane and just society, and that serve the common good. We have done this often in the past, and with great success. We can recall the adoption of the Social Security Act at a time when far too many American seniors were spending their last days in poverty. To this day, this is probably the most effective anti-poverty legislation our country has ever enacted. Or we can think of the success of Lyndon Johnson's Great Society and the anti-poverty programs of the 1960s. While some have questioned their efficacy, it is hard to believe that without these programs the poverty rate in this country would have dropped from 22 percent in 1958 to 11 percent in 1973.

In addressing poverty in America we must remember that this is not something for the "government" alone to deal with because the government is us. As former Vice President and Senator Hubert H. Humphrey is credited with saying, in what is a twentieth-century rendering of the words of the biblical prop-ets: "The moral test of government is how it treats those who are in the dawn of life, the children; those who are in the twilight of life, the aged; and those in the shadows of life, the sick, the needy and the handicapped."[10]

If we are true to our heritage, we will again heed this wise counsel. We must continue the conversation, invent, lead, take up the challenge of *love in truth*. It is up to us to affirm the dignity of each person in this country. We can do it, and we must.

Chapter 7
Acting Anew
Innovative Programs from the Nonprofit Sector

> *When it was evening, the disciples came to him and said,
> "This is a deserted place, and the hour is now late; send
> the crowds away so that they may go into the villages and
> buy food for themselves." Jesus said to them, "They need
> not go away; you give them something to eat." They re-
> plied, "We have nothing here but five loaves and two fish."
> And he said, "Bring them here to me." Then he ordered the
> crowds to sit down on the grass. Taking the five loaves and
> the two fish, he looked up to heaven, and blessed and broke
> the loaves, and gave them to the disciples, and the disciples
> gave them to the crowds. And all ate and were filled; and
> they took up what was left over of the broken pieces, twelve
> baskets full. And those who ate were about five thousand
> men, besides women and children* (Matt. 14:15-21).

I think of this story from the Gospels when I think of the work
that Catholic Charities workers do day in and day out as they
marshal scarce resources and through some miracle of love, caring, and sharing manage to provide for those who flock to them
for help. In reality these miracles are based in a constant flow
of innovation, of testing new ideas, and adopting the successful models of others. This creativity has enabled us to meet the
demands of growing numbers of people in need—an additional
1.25 million in the last two years alone.

We are proud of our ability to meet the growing demands
for services and also humbled by the desperate lives of the peo-

ple who come to us for help. When you really examine what we do, it is not a cause for celebration. Unlike McDonald's, which served its one billionth burger less than ten years after it was founded, our goal is not to increase the number of people we serve. We want to serve fewer people—for the reason that they will no longer need our services.

What we need, of course, is to rethink the services that we as a nation have been providing for those in need. We also need to rethink how those services are delivered, and to assess whether they are leading to self-sufficiency. And if not, what must we do to change our system?

Some Model Programs

During Catholic Charities USA's year-long outreach to our members and their communities, countless examples of innovative programs have surfaced that merit recognition and discussion. Our meetings and on-line forums also have generated ideas that warrant further exploration. We have selected a few of them to profile here (not necessarily all directly affiliated with Catholic Charities USA) in the hope that they will lead to new, innovative solutions to poverty in America. While they currently may be small in scope they potentially are the seeds for resetting America's social landscape.

Step Up Silicon Valley

Step Up Silicon Valley: The Campaign to Cut Poverty in Santa Clara County is a community-based initiative that includes community-based organizations, the public sector, faith communities, and businesses.

The cost of living in Santa Clara County in California is higher than in many other areas in the nation, resulting in a poverty level that is greater than the federal poverty threshold. By using the Family Economic Self-Sufficiency Standard to measure poverty, Step Up Silicon Valley has determined that 25 percent of its residents are living below the poverty level. According to Greg Kepferle, executive director of Catholic Charities of Santa Clara County, nearly half of the low-income people living in Silicon Valley go hungry for some time each month. He estimates that 54 percent of the eligible residents of Santa Clara County do not access the Food Stamp Program, a potential loss of more than $83 million annually in federal assistance. In Santa Clara County the high cost of housing is one of the largest contributors to poverty. In the city of San Jose alone, as many as twenty thousand households may be at risk of homelessness. A worker needs to make $24 an hour and work full time in order to afford the average rent on a two-bedroom apartment. As Kepferle said to the San Jose *Mercury News,*

> It's shameful that in one of the wealthiest areas in one of the wealthiest countries in the world we have people living on the streets, kids that are too hungry to learn, a janitor working two, three jobs and his family is living in a van. We need to help those families because they're already helping themselves as much as they can.[1]

In early 2007, Catholic Charities of Santa Clara County convened a meeting of representatives from local non-profits, social services agencies, businesses, faith-based organizations, and government to discuss how to cut poverty in half by 2020. The result was the creation of Step Up Silicon Valley. Over the course of the next eighteen months, the list of participants grew to more than ninety organizations.

Silicon Valley is known for its entrepreneurial spirit, its drive for innovation, and its ingenuity in solving complex problems. Private and public organizations are strongly committed to caring for the needy and they have a proven track record of making a difference.

Step Up Silicon Valley has developed an action plan to cut poverty by increasing awareness, building partnerships, shaping public policy, increasing private and public funding, and integrating services to better meet the needs of the poor. Step Up Silicon Valley urges local officials, the California Legislature, Congress, and the administration to make decisions on programs based on the goal of reducing poverty. For more on Step Up Silicon Valley, visit www.stepupsv.com.

Time Banks

A Time Bank is a community of people who support each other with their time. Time banking means "spending an hour doing something for somebody in yo ur community." That hour goes into the Time Bank as a Time Dollar, which becomes a Time Dollar to have someone do something for you. "It's a simple idea, but it has powerful ripple effects in building community connections."[2] An example is the Visiting Nurse Service of New York Community Connections TimeBank, where members can earn one "time credit" for every hour of assistance they provide to another member; they then can redeem their credits to receive services for themselves from other members of the TimeBank. As the organization's website describes, "A mother might cook for an elderly neighbor and receive tutoring for her kid. A teen might teach computer skills and receive a guitar lesson." Membership is free and the members include children, teenagers, parents, young adults, and retirees.

Time Banks emerged from the ideas of Edgar Cahn, author and educator, who came up with the concept of "time dollars" as a currency that could replace some of the government spending on social welfare and be used to provide people with needed services. Time Banks now exist in at least twenty-four states and twenty-two countries. For more on Time Banks, visit www. timebanks.org.

Harlem Children's Zone

Over the past twenty years the Harlem Children's Zone has been one of the most successful anti-poverty programs in the country. It offers a unique, holistic approach to rebuilding a community so that its children can stay on track through college and go on to enter the job market. The goal is to create a "tipping point" in the neighborhood so that children are surrounded by an enriching environment of college-oriented peers and supportive adults, a counterweight to "the streets" and a popular culture that glorifies anti-social behavior. In January 2007, the HCZ Project launched its Phase 3, expanding its comprehensive system of programs to nearly one hundred blocks of central Harlem.

President Obama has used the Harlem Children's Zone model to create a new federal program, "Promise Neighborhoods." The president included a $210 million request in his 2011 Department of Education budget to support grants to community-based organizations for the development and implementation of plans for comprehensive Promise Neighborhood programs. Promise Neighborhoods (1) serve the entire neighborhood, with at least 65 percent of the children in that area; (2) create holistic support programs that surround the children throughout their lives—not just in terms of place-based education but also in terms of fitness, personal development, and much more; (3) build community support with residents, institutions, and stakeholders; (4) provide on-going, evaluative review and analysis of program outcomes; and (5) create a culture of success with accountability, passion, leadership, and teamwork. For more on the Harlem Children's Zone, visit www.hcz.org.

The Box Project

The Box Project, founded in 1962, was born out of the Civil Rights movement to match volunteer sponsors—families, individuals, churches, organizations, businesses—from across the United States with families living in poverty in the rural South. Its approach is to help people out of poverty through direct contact and personal relationships.

The Box Project pairs sponsors with carefully screened individuals or families that need financial help. Sponsors communicate and send letters and boxes of needed goods directly to the families they are matched with, developing a one-to-one experience. As the families come to know each other, trust and friendships grow that provide a positive and valuable experience for both the recipient and the sponsor. The sponsor provides direct contributions to the needy family, such as non-perishable food items and special clothing, and costs the sponsor approximately $50 per month.

Recipients are screened and recommended by non-profit service agencies and pay a $10 yearly membership fee. They must qualify for assistance, live in a county designated as "rural," and earn less than 150 percent of the federal poverty guidelines. Sponsors are encouraged to learn as much as they can about their family and where they live: services in the area, educational and job opportunities, and other options that might be accessed to help the recipient family move toward a better level of self-sufficiency.

The Box Project currently serves carefully selected areas of rural poverty in the Mississippi Delta, on South Dakota Native American reservations, in the Appalachia region of West Virginia and Kentucky, and in rural regions of Maine.

In 2009 the Box Project merged with The Community Foundation of Northwest Mississippi. For more information on the Box Project, visit www.cfnm.org/.

Wheels for Work

The Wheels for Work Program of Catholic Charities of the Diocese of Albany, New York, is a public-private-NGO partnership that brings the resources of the community together to help improve lives. Families in the community often are trapped in impoverished conditions because they lack transportation to get to work.

Wheels for Work receives vehicles donated by the general public. Each vehicle is checked at a licensed automotive shop that makes the repairs needed to make the vehicle road ready, and it is then given to a family whose household income falls within 200 percent of the federal poverty guidelines. The Wheels for Work Program works collaboratively with local leaders, the business community, public policymakers, members of faith-based communities, and civic groups to lend a committed hand to families who live in poverty.

Twelve local Albany businesses serve as formal partners and provide towing, auto mechanic services, auto body work, auto clinics, driver instruction, insurance, banking, and emergency road service. It began as a pilot project in 2001 and was subsequently funded through the New York State Department of Labor and then through the New York State Office of Temporary and Disability Assistance. Participants of the Wheels for Work initiative have increased their income and personal assets.

Earthworks Urban Farm

Finding safe and nutritious foods continues to be a challenge for low-income families in many communities across the United

States. In recent years, some local community providers have turned to community gardens as a way to expand access to fresh fruits and vegetables. The promotion and creation of multiple community gardens in urban areas has the potential to systematically improve local food access. Blighted areas are transformed into verdant gardens. These areas are not only aesthetically pleasing, they also provide food to the community, empower local people, and witness to the creation of a just food system.

The Earthworks Urban Farm provides an excellent model. Detroit, on the whole, has seen a dramatic increase in community gardens. Out of the over three hundred community gardens in the Detroit area, the Earthworks Urban Farm is one of the most successful.

In 1997, a Capuchin brother of the Province of St. Joseph in Detroit started a garden at his workplace, the Capuchin Soup Kitchen. The kitchen serves two thousand meals per day to the poor who lack basic human needs. That small plot of land grew into the Earthworks Urban Farm project, an exercise in social justice and a means of restoring respectful relationships between individuals with the land and food it produces. Each year, farm volunteers pick hundreds of pounds of grapes, gooseberries, black and red raspberries, elderberries, and currants that are turned into jam and sold at local farmers markets and area stores.

In 2003 Earthworks Urban Farm/Capuchin Soup Kitchen joined The Greening of Detroit, Detroit Agriculture Network, and Michigan State University to create the Garden Resource Program (GRP) to provide residents with the supplies and resources they need to grow food in the city.

By 2010 GRP was providing support to more than 875 urban gardens and farms in the Detroit area. GRP members receive seeds and Detroit-grown transplants and "become part of a growing network of growers and advocates working to promote and encourage urban agriculture and a thriving local food system in the City of Detroit."[3] For more information, please visit www.cskdetroit.org/, www.detroitagriculture.org/GRP.

The Dinner Garden

The Dinner Garden is a nonprofit organization that is based on a simple idea—if people can grow their own food, they will not have to depend on public assistance for food support. Gardening techniques have evolved to the point that gardening is accessible to people who have no money for supplies or who don't own land. A few pots on a terrace or windowsill will do.

The Dinner Garden, based in San Antonio, supplies seeds, gardening supplies, and gardening advice free of charge to anyone in the United States. Each gardener gets five to six varieties of seeds, enough to start a garden for a family of four. In 2009 to early 2010 they had given more than 45,000 seed packs to gardeners in all fifty states, and had a waiting list of over 15,000 people waiting to get seeds. Seed packs are sent to distribution sites that are set up with businesses all over the country. They also will mail seeds free of charge to the gardeners, even though each seed pack costs $1.79 to create and ship.

The impact can be tremendous. The Dinner Garden's website claims that

> a head of lettuce from one seed costs between $2.00 to $3.00. A pound of squash will cost you $2.00 to $3.00. One squash seed will produce several pounds of squash. Tomatoes run $1.00 to $2.00 per pound. One seed will produce around 40 pounds of tomatoes. Carrots cost about $1.00 per pound, or about $.20 a carrot.
>
> 250 Beefsteak tomato seeds cost us $9.00. We pay

$18.00 for 216,000 carrot seeds. Lettuce is $16.00 for 372,000 seeds. 7,350 squash seeds cost $18.00. That equates to paying $9.00 for 10,000 pounds of tomatoes, $18.00 for 216,000 carrots, $16.00 for 372,000 heads of lettuce, and $18.00 for 110,250 pounds of squash. For this example, the retail price for all this produce is $1,263,825. So for $61 in seeds, we can grow about $1.3 million worth of vegetables.[4]

The organization provides information for gardeners on its website about how to harvest seeds from the produce they grow so they will have seeds for the next planting season. The Dinner Garden is a cost-effective, sustainable solution to hunger. It has been time tested and proved viable through the Victory Garden campaign in the early 1900s. Growing a Dinner Garden can increase food security, improve nutrition, and decrease dependence on public assistance. More information is available at www.dinnergarden.org/.

City Greens

In 2009 Catholic Charities in St. Louis took an overgrown, cluttered urban lot and built a garden as a pilot for its program called City Greens, a program designed to make affordable fresh produce available to lower-income families. The garden is worked by a rotating team of volunteers, and the St. Louis Land Reutilization Authority leases the plot to nearby Catholic Charities for $1 a year. The raised beds allow for crops to be grown in clean, compost-based soil.

City Greens at the Midtown Center is a hybrid of a farmers' market and a fresh food co-op. Produce grown on the plot is sold along with produce from a group of area farmers. The market is aimed at neighborhood residents but is open to anyone. Participation is free for families with annual incomes of $30,000 or less. Those with larger incomes pay a fee of $60 for ten market visits or $100 for twenty-four visits. The membership fees help City Greens plan their budget and make the food affordable.

Frugality through innovation is a key practice in the garden plot. Volunteers learn to make paper pots for starting plants by wrapping paper around wine bottles. And when a local farmer brought daikon radishes to the market last year, a volunteer developed a recipe for daikon coleslaw to show neighborhood residents what to do with the radishes. Additional information is available at www.ccstl.org/.

Recipe for Success

Since 1984, the New Hampshire Food Bank (NHFB), a program of Catholic Charities of New Hampshire, has provided food to qualified nonprofit programs serving the hungry throughout New Hampshire. The New Hampshire Food Bank is the only food warehouse distribution center in the state. Last year, close to six million pounds of donated and surplus food was distributed to more than four hundred pantries, soup kitchens, shelters, day care centers, senior citizen homes, and substance abuse treatment centers across the state.

In addition to food distribution, NHFB developed an innovative outreach program called Recipe for Success, a four-part program that combines job training, nutrition education, fresh food collection, and a community garden to help serve people in the community who are at risk of hunger.

Its Culinary Job Training Program helps unemployed and underemployed people gain the skills and experience necessary to seek employment in the food service industry and provides prepared meals to thousands of needy people in New Hampshire. Culinary students learn marketable skills ranging from efficient kitchen practices and fundamentals to serving and meal presentation. They also receive training in basic financial skills, resume writing, and interview techniques. Trainees prepare meals that provide at least one hundred meals per day for the Manchester Boys & Girls Club, as well as meals in bulk that are frozen and distributed to other agencies.

Another of its programs, Operation Frontline, connects families with resources and information to develop the skills to make healthy food choices, prepare tasty meals on a limited budget, and make the most out of their food dollar.

In a partnership with supermarkets across the state, staff at NHFB's Fresh Rescue program collect fresh meat (including poultry, beef, and fish) that would otherwise be disposed of every week. In 2009, the Food Bank collected a total of 215,357 pounds of protein through this program.

Under the guidance of the Garden Coordinator, volunteers at the Production Garden plant, tend, grow, and harvest fresh vegetables for use by Operation Frontline and the Culinary Job Training Program, as well as for distribution to member agencies.

St. Leo Campus for Veterans

The St. Leo Campus, located in Chicago's Auburn Gresham neighborhood, is an initiative to keep veterans safe and off the streets. The St. Leo Campus includes Catholic Charities' St. Leo Residence, the Auburn Gresham Community Based Outpatient Clinic, the St. Leo Veterans Garden, and the Pope John Paul II Residence, which provides apartment housing for persons with physical disabilities.

The ultimate goal on the St. Leo Campus is self-sufficiency. With stable housing and wrap-around services, homeless veterans can make the transition to self-sufficiency. By receiving treatment for their physical and mental health problems and support in maintaining recovery, finding employment, and building life skills, formerly homeless veterans can live independently with dignity.

The St. Leo Residence consists of 141 furnished studio apartments and offers expansive common recreational space, a fitness room, and multipurpose meeting rooms that can be used for meetings about veteran-specific issues, including Alcoholics Anonymous and Narcotics Anonymous. An on-site library and computer lab with internet access provide residents with invaluable resources for employment, health care, and housing. While at the Residence, veterans receive case management assistance to help coordinate the array of services that are located within the Residence, nearby at the Department of Veterans Affairs' Auburn Gresham Community Based Outpatient Clinic, and the adjoining Resource Center. The clinic provides medical care, employment training, and other support services to residents of the St. Leo Campus as well as to an estimated twenty thousand additional veterans residing in the surrounding community.

The Pope John Paul II Residence at St. Leo's, opened in 2007, is specially designed for persons with physical disabilities who meet HUD's income requirements, are eighteen years of age or older, and have a physical impairment that substantially impedes their ability to live independently. Preference is given to applicants who currently have no means of housing, or reside in substandard housing, or currently are paying more than 50 percent of their income for rent and utilities. All rents are subsidized under a rental assistance program. Eligible households pay no more than 30 percent of their adjusted gross income for rent and utilities.

Located directly across from the St. Leo Residence, the St. Leo Veterans Garden contains a beautiful fountain and five distinct areas that honor the different branches of the military.

These initiatives are designed to help formerly homeless veterans achieve self-sufficiency and prevent homelessness through employment services and through the provision of affordable housing for senior veterans.

B Corporations

B Corporations, also known as benefit corporations (as described previously in chapter 5), help cut poverty by enabling for-profit corporations to maximize social and environmental good along with earning profits. For-profit publicly traded corporations have a primary responsibility to maximize profit for their shareholders. The current corporation and tax laws at state and federal governments present a barrier for corporations with a double and/or triple bottom line (social good + environmental sustainability + profit) by subordinating the broader mission of these corporations to a single dimension: economic profit to shareholders. There is a movement among businesses with a social purpose to change state corporation laws (Maryland, Vermont, New York, Colorado, North Carolina, Washington, Oregon, and Pennsylvania) to enable corporations with triple bottom lines to balance the profit motive with social good. Maryland recently changed its law to create B corporations: for-profit corporations that can give half their money to charity, create social businesses that support people in poverty, be carbon neutral, and in general benefit the common good. For more information on B corporations, see www.bcorporation.net.

The Village at King Farm

The Village at King Farm is a Workforce Housing Community in Montgomery County, Maryland, developed to provide affordable housing for municipal employees and other income-qualified workers. The community is located close to major roads and transit hubs and provides home-buyers with household incomes between 71 percent and 120 percent of the median income (between $48,500 and $128,500) in the Washington, D.C. area an opportunity to own a home at below-market prices.

King Farm is one example of workforce housing, a relatively new concept developed by local governments and planners to address the need for affordable housing for the area's "critical workforce" (for example, police officers, firemen, teachers, nurses, emergency medical technicians, and municipal and corporate support personnel), ensuring that these community service providers can live near where they work. For this population, home prices, often based on mortgage, interest, taxes, and insurance, should account for no more than 30 percent of household income. Workforce housing is often built in rehabilitated warehouses and/or in foreclosed housing either in or near retail centers. The development of workforce housing enables communities to establish more affordable housing ownership options for working families, which helps them break out of rent cycles with the uncertainties of rent increases.

Christian Community Services: Family Mentoring and Life Skills Education

Nashville's Christian Community Services, Inc. (CCSI) uses mentoring relationships to help underserved families attain self-sufficiency. Families currently receiving government assistance are paired with mentor families and together they attend financial management classes and counseling, life skills classes, and family mentoring. Their goal is to become self-sufficient within five years.

CCSI depends on volunteer mentors who are paired with a family through the Mentoring Toward Independence program. Mentors encourage families and, by modeling Christian values, their relationship becomes a powerful means of transforming life-long patterns of behavior, encouraging spiritual, emotional, and financial self-sufficiency. Mentors share dinner with their mentees, talk about their week, and then attend classes. They also spend time weekly catching up with the mentees outside of the Tuesday night class.

While participating in the program, the families are required to contribute monthly into an Individual Development Account (IDA) that is matched two-for-one up to $5,000. The savings can be used to purchase a home, pursue higher education, or start a business.

Because a goal of the program is to create a legacy of self-sufficiency, CCSI provides guidance, homework assistance, and encouragement to preschool and school-age children while their parents attend the life skills class.

According to the organization's website, seventy-one CCSI families purchased their first homes and moved out of public or government-subsidized housing, resulting in annual property tax revenues of approximately $78,000.[5]

Because the program relies heavily on volunteers, it could be replicated in communities across the country with a minimal staff infrastructure. See http://www.ccsinashville.org/.

Individual Development Account Collaborative

The Individual Development Account Collaborative of Louisiana (IDA) consisted of educational and financial institutions, community- and faith-based organizations, workforce organizations, social service providers, and public agencies that worked to encourage low-income families to save money by offering a matched savings account.

The IDA Collaborative, now closed, had some noteworthy accomplishments. Its main goal was to help low-income families create and maintain a goal and succeed in saving toward a home, post-secondary education, or a business start-up. The IDA would partner with local banks to open bank accounts for the individuals. Individuals who were approved were then required to take financial education classes, and no money could be withdrawn from the account without the signature of the individual and the program manager. Upon reaching a goal, the IDA would match funds saved up to $1,000.

The IDA, which was sponsored by Tulane University, was closed due to the financial impact of Hurricane Katrina. But while it was in business 300 people bought homes, 151 became graduates of higher education, and 157 small businesses were started.

Inmates Helping Inmates

Inmates Helping Inmates encourages state correctional facilities to allow adult education departments in local colleges to train qualified prison inmates (carefully selected by the prison) to become one-on-one reading tutors for illiterate prison inmates. The experience is personally rewarding for the inmate tutor in terms of feelings of self-worth and accomplishment, and it is extremely important to the illiterate inmate student as it opens doors of employment and social acceptance once he or she is released. Such programs, which can reduce inmate recidivism by 40 percent, result in saved state resources. A real advantage of such programs is that they require no real investment and cost next to nothing.

The School Archive Project

An innovative program to prevent students from dropping out of school helps students to focus on their own future. The School Archive Project includes a ten-year time capsule and a class reunion plan designed to help students visualize their own story and appreciate their natural ability to change their lives through work.

The first School Archive was a 350-pound vault, bolted to the floor of the Quintanilla Middle School (near Dallas) lobby in 2005; the vault functioned as the time-capsule. It holds letters written by eighth-grade students to themselves. These letters tell about their lives, their dreams, their achievements, and their ten-year goals. Holding their letters, the students pose for a photo with their class in front of the School Archive and then, one by one, they each place their envelope into the Archive.

Students know they will return to retrieve these letters at their class reunion ten years later. At that reunion they know they will be also be invited to speak with then current students about their recommendations for success. They are warned to prepare for questions from the younger students such as, "Would you do anything differently if you were thirteen again?" High schools that have received the Archive Project students since the project started have improved their graduation and upper-grade enrollment rates much more dramatically than the other thirty high schools within the Dallas school district.

Social Enterprise Tax Credits

Social Enterprise Tax Credits could provide for-profit businesses with an incentive to invest in public-benefit enterprises in a manner similar to the highly successful affordable housing tax credit program.

One of the key struggles in the Campaign to Reduce Poverty in America is how to engage the business community in the campaign and how to enlist its support in reducing poverty. The idea for social enterprise tax credits comes from affordable housing development. Expanding the concept of affordable housing tax credits to other areas of the social good, such as food, health care, education, social services, and income development, would create the potential to leverage large sums of capital investments in these areas. Investors would receive a tax credit for their investment over a period of time. A tax credit rather than a simple tax deduction would give a greater advantage to the corporation and provide a larger benefit to the social enterprise.

Examples include capital investments in projects that are scalable and replicable and thus have the potential to reach large numbers of low-income individuals, such as (1) developing and distributing below-market-price medicines and medical supplies; (2) creating access to information technologies for low-income communities; (3) expanding community-based sustainable agriculture; (4) sustaining, creating, and/or expanding social businesses that develop living-wage jobs; (5) developing and distributing low-cost alternative energy to low-income communities; and (6) developing high-quality affordable schools in low-income communities.

To be eligible for tax credit financing, projects would be required to demonstrate a public benefit; in other words, a certain percentage of beneficiaries would qualify for a price reduction based on incomes being lower than median income levels for the region.

Community Warehouse

Community Warehouse is a Portland-based 501(c)(3) nonprofit agency that collects and redistributes donated furniture and household goods to individuals and families in need. The organization uses a network of nonprofit social services agencies throughout northwest Oregon and southwest Washington to distribute basic household items that help individuals and families create a home. The Warehouse is supplied solely by donations and encourages neighborhoods and individuals to organize donation drives.

Community Warehouse clients include women escaping domestic violence, the elderly, people with mental and physical disabilities, refugee families, youths and adults recovering from substance abuse, and the working poor. It serves an average of two hundred individuals per week.

One local resident held a "Gadget Exchange" party for friends who looked through closets, drawers, basements, and garages for household items they did not need or for which they have duplicates. At the party they exchanged their wares for one item brought by someone else. The rest of the goods were donated to the Community Warehouse. The idea of a Community Warehouse combined with Gadget Exchanges gets individuals involved who might not otherwise think to give away their unused items. For more information see http://communitywarehouse.org.

St. Elizabeth's Health Center

St. Elizabeth's Health Center in Tucson was founded in 1961 as a faith-based community health center to provide medical, dental, and health care for the uninsured and underserved in southern Arizona. Today, St. Elizabeth's annually serves over twenty thousand patients of all ages who do not have medical and/or dental insurance. St. Elizabeth's operates on a sliding-scale fee basis with volunteer physicians and dentists available to help keep the costs of care affordable.

St. Elizabeth's has been acknowledged by the Arizona Department of Health Services as a "gold standard" in providing affordable care for uninsured working families. Its unique model of care is based on a partnership between a small paid staff and over 165 volunteer physicians, dentists, and other health-care professionals.

St. Elizabeth's continues to develop and offer innovative services such as telemedicine and telepsychiatry, along with group-care models, cooking demonstrations, community health workers (*promotora*), neighborhood outreach, and alternative medicine options for patients. St. Elizabeth's Health Center partners with many community hospitals and organizations to assure that patients needing medical and/or dental care have access to the highest quality of care.

Jessie Albert Memorial Dental Center

Adequate dental care is one of the most pervasive health-care challenges facing children in the United States. At the same time, early intervention can reduce long-term dental costs and serious health crises for low-income families. According to a report by the U.S. Surgeon General,

[T]here are striking disparities in dental disease by income. Poor children suffer twice as many dental cavities as their more affluent peers, and their disease is more likely to be untreated. . . . One out of four children in America is born into poverty, and children living below the poverty line . . . have more severe and untreated decay.[6]

The report also notes that "more than 51 million school hours are lost each year to dental-related illness. Poor children suffer nearly 12 times more restricted-activity days than children from higher-income families."

Catholic Charities of Maine developed a unique program to expand dental health care to low-income families in the state. The Jessie Albert Memorial Dental Center provides affordable, quality, comprehensive dental and orthodontic services to children, adolescents, and adults. This includes preventive, restorative, orthodontic, and emergency dental services. The center also is involved in multiple outreach programs that provide free dental care for children from volunteer area dentists, and it provides space and equipment in the evenings for the free dental care for low-income adults. The center is committed to providing affordable dental care to its patients; if the patient has no insurance, payment is made according to a sliding fee scale.

The dental health program provided services to 3,982 children and young adults in 2008. The program was developed through a partnership between the state government, community organizations, local businesses, and dental insurers in the state. The partnership has grown into a unique, cost-effective, community-based dental health practice that provides comprehensive dental services to working families.

Partnership for Health Care Workers

The Partnership for Health Care Workers is a proposal by Fr. Michael Boland, CEO of Catholic Charities of Chicago, to leverage training resources by developing a program between the non-profit community and for-profit hospitals to decrease the number of vacancies for health-care workers in the Chicago area and to increase the opportunities for skilled employment in local communities. This approach would create training and employment opportunities for unskilled workers by training individuals for existing jobs. Over the long term it would also improve access to health-care services in disadvantaged communities.

Fr. Boland suggested a pilot initiative between Catholic Charities agencies and Catholic hospitals to test this model. As part of this model, individuals being trained would also receive all needed services in order to be successful, including housing assistance, food, quality child care, transportation, and counseling.

Together We Care Act

The most recent U.S. Census Bureau data shows that there are more than 30 million senior citizens in the United States today. It is estimated that by 2030, this number will increase to 72 million.[7] According to a 2006 survey conducted by the AARP, many older residents of subsidized public housing experience some level of frailty or disability—more so than same-age residents of unsubsidized housing.[8] While "the goal for young families is to enable them to move on to unsubsidized housing . . . the goal for older persons is to allow them to age in place and remain out of expensive institutional settings."[9] Compounding this problem is the fact that many families, particularly those with low or no income, are unable to care for their older family members on their own.

In 2009 Rep. Nydia Velazquez of New York proposed the "Together We Care Act" that would create a program to train public housing residents as health-care aides for older persons living in public or subsidized housing who cannot afford health care. At the same time the program would also create jobs for those who also live in public housing. The trainees would then be able to provide home health-care assistance to other residents in need of such services and help them remain in their homes and avoid unnecessary or premature institutionalization. Home health aide programs can average seventy-five hours of training, including practical training under supervision.

Gateway to Financial Fitness

Gateway to Financial Fitness is a unique financial literacy program that helps low-income families overcome barriers to financial health and stability. The greatest barrier for this population is often a lack of information about financial matters. The program consists of five aspects of personal financial management: (1) values, goal-setting, and spending; (2) taxes, record-keeping, and contracts; (3) credit; (4) financial institutions, saving, and investing; and (5) insurance and benefits.

Gateway to Financial Fitness is run by the Catholic Charities Housing Resource Center (CCHRC), an agency of Catholic Charities of the Archdiocese of St. Louis. In addition to its financial management learning program, CCHRC joined a group of eight nonprofits to establish the CHOICES Federal Credit Union in 2006. CHOICES is one of a handful of credit unions in the St. Louis region devoted to meeting the financial needs of low-income people. CHOICES was created to give low-income people easy access to affordable financial services and promote healthy savings for the future. A part-time manager and volunteers run CHOICES, which is housed at a local community development agency. A $10 deposit into a savings account creates a membership. Direct deposit and/or payroll deductions are used to build savings. Members can obtain low-cost loans to purchase a new or used car, consolidate debt, or buy consumer goods. Members also can apply for a secured credit card, which has a limit no larger than the amount of funds in their savings account. For more information, visit www.ccstl.org.

The Challenge of These Programs

These are just a few of the hundreds of innovative and effective programs that are being developed in cities, towns, and states across the country. They can serve as models for other communities to reduce factors that contribute to poverty, but they can be models only if their inspiration is shared. As Jesus said to the crowds in the mountains of Galilee, "No one after lighting a lamp puts it under the bushel basket, but on the lampstand, and it gives light to all in the house" (Matt. 5:15).

We intend to be that light.

Chapter 8
To Think and Act Anew

It came upon the midnight clear,
That glorious song of old,
From angels bending near the earth,
To touch their harps of gold:
"Peace on the earth, goodwill to men,
From heaven's all-gracious King."
The world in solemn stillness lay,
To hear the angels sing. . . .

And ye, beneath life's crushing load,
Whose forms are bending low,
Who toil along the climbing way
With painful steps and slow,
Look now! for glad and golden hours
come swiftly on the wing.
O rest beside the weary road,
And hear the angels sing!

—Edmund Sears, "It Came Upon a Midnight Clear" (1849)

Each Christmas we revisit the scene of the Nativity: the babe in the manger, the stars in the sky on that midnight clear, shepherds watching over their flocks, cattle lowing. It sounds bucolic. But imagine what a huge disruption this was—all of a sudden a multitude of angels appeared, tearing through the veil that separates heaven from earth, and over all of the chaos and din that is life on earth, they sang one clear song from heaven: "Christ our savior is born." It was a cry of help and hope.

This wee child, born into such strangely dramatic and yet humble circumstances, came to bring us an urgent word from heaven. Love God, and love your neighbor as yourself. Not simply a request or a suggestion. This is what we are mandated to do.

Today we stand in the midst of what we experience as chaos on multiple fronts. We have lost faith in many of our institutions—banks, government, corporations—to effect change for the better, to be able to solve big problems such as reinvigorating the economy or saving the Gulf of Mexico. We can barely think about the poor.

The Christian Mandate

When it comes to the poor, we are not mandated to focus on obstacles to tackling a difficult problem or to retreat in despair when we do not immediately achieve our goal. Instead, we are mandated to care for the least among us. Our current situation presents us with an incredible opportunity to bring about change that, as we rebuild our nation, will leave no one behind. We stand at a crossroads that presents us with a once-in-a-generation chance to defeat the poverty that is both a personal tragedy for millions and a public disgrace that eats away at the fiber of our nation.

The basic question before us is what kind of society we want to be. We are a creative, talented, and gifted people who are rich in resources. If we put our minds to it, we can reshape the social contract of our country so that no person is left out or left behind. We should not be content with maintaining the status quo. To bring about the dramatic change that reflects our faith and commitment, we need to "think and act anew."

But our obligation does not stop there. As people of faith, we will not get it right until we acknowledge that everyone is our sister or brother—even those whose appearance or behavior is unappealing to us. For deep inside of them lies the sacred image of our God who asks nothing more of us than "to do justice, and to love kindness, and to walk humbly with your God" (Mic. 6:8).

Many of the words of Pope John Paul II speak to us even now with a directness that cuts to the very heart of the matter:

> How can it be that even today there are still people dying of hunger? Condemned to illiteracy? Lacking the most basic medical care? Without a roof over their heads? . . . Christians must learn to make their act of faith in Christ by discerning his voice in the cry for help that rises from this world of poverty (*Millennio Ineunte*, 50).

Over the years the Catholic bishops of the United States have been just as direct in calling us to a vision of the Church that engages society in a way that promotes the values of the Gospel. They encourage us to use moral persuasion to show that we are all called to adhere to basic values that transcend any particular race or government.

As Catholics, we must come together with a common conviction that we can no longer tolerate the moral scandal of poverty in our land and so much hunger and deprivation in our world. As believers, we can debate how best to overcome these realities, but we must be united in our determination to do so. Our faith teaches us that poor people are not issues or problems but sisters and brothers in God's one human family (U.S. Conference of Catholic Bishops, *A Place at the Table*, 2002).

Pope Benedict XVI states that our development as people *"depends, above all, on a recognition that the human race is a single family* working together in true communion, not simply a group of subjects who happen to live side by side" (*Caritas in Veritate*, 53). He urges that "a new trajectory of thinking is needed" for us to fully comprehend what it means to live and work as one family (53).

We must see clearly that the eradication of poverty is a personal, moral mandate for each of us. I believe we can create an economy that provides equal opportunity for all who can work, and a society that supports and cares for those who truly cannot. But we must regain our faith in our ability—and in the ability of our institutions—to bring about change and to solve big problems. We can do this by coming together as one family and making the decisions that a family would make to take care of its own. It will require us to think and act anew. As St. Paul said, "Do not be conformed to this world, but be transformed by the renewing of your minds, so that you may discern what is the will of God—what is good and acceptable and perfect" (Rom. 12:2).

And so the conversation needs to continue. We must once more tap into our creativity and devise big, innovative, twenty-first century ideas that will reshape the twenty-first century social landscape of our country and be based on values that truly represent the best of our human nature. We are by nature drawn to the good; the challenges of today demand that we aim for the best. Let us again bring the economic together with the social in an ethical way that speaks loudly of our common priorities.

Our Faith Is Profoundly Social

As the U.S. Conference of Catholic Bishops noted in its 1993 statement, *Communities of Salt and Light: Reflections on the Social Mission of the Parish*, "The central message is simple: our faith is profoundly social. We cannot be called truly 'Catholic' unless we hear and heed the Church's call to serve those in need and work for justice and peace."

Many have heeded this call before us.

In the 1930s Dorothy Day looked around her and started the Catholic Worker movement, creating houses of hospitality for those who were homeless. When asked "Didn't Jesus say that the poor would be with us always?" she would reply: "Yes, but we are not content that there should be so many of them." Today there are more than 185 Catholic Worker Communities in the world, with 168 in the United States.[1]

In 1961 a young John Fitzgerald Kennedy stood in the cold January wind and rallied our nation. "Ask not what your country can do for you," he said, "ask what you can do for your country . . . knowing that here on earth God's work must truly be our own."

And on September 11, 2001, Father Mychal Judge and hundreds of firefighters, police officers, and rescue workers sped off toward the World Trade Center on a mission of loving service from which they would not return.

As Easter people we must believe that in those and countless other bold expressions of Catholic charity the angels descended once again from heaven, urging us to be not afraid, reminding us of the words of the risen Christ: "to obey everything that I have commanded you" (Matt. 28:20). When we are called, we must respond. I believe we are called now to think and act anew about how we as individuals and businesses and organizations and governments can feed our hungry, give drink to our thirsty, welcome strangers, clothe those who are naked, care for our sick, provide a good education for our children, and ensure a roof over the head of every man, woman, and child in America.

I challenge our faithful, our teachers, our leaders, and our neighbors to join Catholic Charities to engage in a national discussion that makes ending poverty in America our top priority.

We are all on a journey toward God. May our actions together be grounded in the criteria upon which we ultimately will be judged, so that we may hear the words of the king: "Come, you that are blessed by my Father, inherit the kingdom prepared for you from the foundation of the world" (Matt. 25:34).

As we will it, so shall the future be.

Notes

Chapter 2: The Faces of the Poor Are Familiar

1. Mark R. Rank, "Rethinking the Scope and Impact of Poverty in the United States," *Connecticut Public Interest Law Journal* 6, no. 2 (Spring/Summer 2007): 170-71.

2. Ellen O'Brien, Ke Bin Wu, and David Baer, *Older Americans in Poverty: A Snapshot*, prepared by the AARP Public Policy Institute, April 2010, http://assets.aarp.org/ (accessed June 10, 2010).

3. http://www.bls.gov/cps/cpswp2007.pdf.

4. David Goldman, "1 in 6 Americans Goes Hungry: Government Report Shows 15% of Americans Had Trouble Putting Food on the Table—A Record High," November 16, 2009, http://money.cnn.com/.

5. Bill Bishop, "Poverty Rate Jumps in Rural America," *Main Street Economics*, November 23, 2009, http://www.dailyyonder.com/.

6. Barry T. Hirsch and David A. MacPherson, "How Unions Help Bring Low-Wage Workers Out of Poverty," Union Membership and Earnings Data Book, BNA, 2010, http://www.aflcio.org/ (accessed June 4, 2010); "The 2009 Poverty Guidelines for the 48 Contiguous States and the District of Columbia," *Federal Register* 74, no. 14 (January 23, 2009), 4199-4201. Prepared by the AFL-CIO.

7. Ibid.

8. Bryan Mitchell, "More Troops Relying on Food Stamps," July 22, 2009, http://www.military.com/.

9. Jason De Parle, "Families Struggle to Afford Food, Survey Finds," *The New York Times*, January 26, 2010.

10. Bureau of Labor Statistics, as quoted by "United States Unemployment Rate," http://www.tradingeconomics./ (accessed June 4, 2010).

11. The Associated Press, "Seniors in Poverty at 19%, New Study Shows: Revised Formula Depicts Americans 65 and Older in Greater Peril Than Previously Believed," September 4, 2009, http://www.cbsnews.com/.

12. Carl Hulse, "Senators End Impasse on Extending Unemployment Benefits," *The New York Times*, April 12, 2010.

13. AARP Press Center, "Last Decade Spelled Disaster for Older Workers," March 3, 2010 http://www.aarp.org/.

14. Justin Lahart, "Manufacturing Capacity Going...," *The Wall Street Journal*, May 17, 2010.

15. Peter S. Goodman, "The New Poor: Despite Signs of Recovery, Chronic Joblessness Rises," *The New York Times*, February 20, 2010.

16. Catholic Charities USA, "Snapshot Survey, First Quarter 2010 Social Services on the Edge: Where Is the Recovery?" http://www.catholiccharitiesusa.org/ (accessed June 4, 2010).

17. Ibid.

Chapter 3: The Dignity and Importance of Each Person

1. Rachel Naomi Remen, *My Grandfather's Blessings: Stories of Strength, Refuge, and Belonging* (New York: Riverhead Trade, 2001), 86 (adapted); and Meir Tamari and Moses Maimonides, "Maimonides' Ladder of Tzedakah: The Best Forms of Charity Make the Recipient Self-sufficient," in *The Challenge of Wealth: A Jewish Perspective on Earning and Spending Money* (Lanham, MD: Jason Aronson, Inc., 1995). Reprinted with permission of the publisher, as posted on www.myjewishlearning.com

Chapter 4: Charity and Justice

1. Walter Brueggemann, "Voices of the Night—Against Justice," in *To Act Justly, Love Tenderly, Walk Humbly: An Agenda for Ministers*, Walter Brueggemann, Sharon Parks, and Thomas H. Groome, eds. (New York: Paulist Press, 1986; reprint, Eugene, OR: Wipf & Stock Publishers, 1997), 5.

2. "Chef Adds Special Ingredient to D.C. Soup Kitchen," NPR, August 10, 2008, www.npr.org/.

3. "60 Minutes Features José Andrés, DCCK," May 4, 2010, as quoted on www.dccentralkitchen.org

Chapter 5: The Common Good and Free Markets

1. As quoted by "Parables," http://www.newadvent.org/ (accessed June 9, 2010): "The Talents" (Matthew 25:14-30), "The Pounds or the Minae" (Luke 19:11-27).

2. About Us, "A Short History of Grameen Bank," http://www.grameen-info.org/ (accessed June 9, 2010).

3. Grameen Bank at a Glance, 4.0, "97 Percent Women," April 2010, www.grameen-info.org.

4. "Professor Yunus Receives Presidential Medal of Freedom," http://www.grameen-info.org/ (accessed June 9, 2010).

5. Michelle Nichols, "Bank for the Poor Hopes to Teach Wall Street a Lesson," May 17, 2010, http://abcnews.go.com/.

6. "Method of Action," www.grameen-info.org/.

7. Franklin D. Roosevelt, "The Forgotten Man," Radio Address air date April 7, 1932, Albany, NY, as quoted by "The Forgotten Man," http://www.teachingamericanhistory.org/ (accessed June 9, 2010).

8. The Aspen Institute Business and Society Program, "A Closer Look at Business Education: Bottom of the Pyramid," June 2007, http://www.beyondgreypinstripes.org/.

9. Israel Moreno Barceló, "Patrimonio Hoy," August 28, 2008, http://www.chamberpost.com/.

10. "Corporate Info," www.toms.com/corporate-info/.

11. Christina Binkley, "Charity Gives Shoe Brand Extra Shine," *The Wall Street Journal*, April 1, 2010.

12. Amy Uelmen, "In the Market for Humanity," *America*, November 30, 2009, http://www.americamagazine.org/.

13. http://www.edc-online.org/.

14. Sarah Mundell, "The EoC at Seton Hall University," May 21, 2010, http://www.edc-online.org/.

15. Jessie Abrams, "Encyclical Brings Light to Economy of Communion Movement," *Catholic News Service*, August 12, 2009.

16. Anne Field, "Not Only for Profit," April 27, 2010, http://trueslant.com/.

17. Evergreen Lodge, "About Us: Youth Program," http://www.evergreenlodge.com/ (accessed June 10, 2009).

18. John Tozzi, "Turning Nonprofits into For-Profits," *Business Week*, June 15, 2009.

19. Greyston Bakery Inc., "Our Social Mission: Vision Statements," http://www.greystonbakery.com/ (accessed June 10, 2010).

Chapter 6: A Nation That Cares for Everyone

1. "Legislative History: Social Security Act of 1935," from www.ssa.gov/history/35actpre.html (accessed June 12, 2010).

2. National Poverty Center, University of Michigan Gerald R. Ford School of Public Policy, "Poverty in the United States: Frequently Asked Questions," http://www.npc.umich.edu/poverty/ (accessed June 14, 2010).

3. Jessie Willis, "How We Measure Poverty: A History and Brief Overview," February 2000, http://www.ocpp.org/.

4. Report by the Commission on the Measurement of Economic Performance and Social Progress, Professor Joseph E. Stiglitz, Chair, Columbia University; Professor Amartya Sen, Chair Adviser, Harvard University; and Professor Jean-Paul Fitoussi, Coordinator of the Commission, IEP.

5. Renee Roth, "The Welfare Cliff," *The Boston Globe*, March 19, 2010, http://www.boston.com/.

6. Ibid.

7. Insight Center for Community Economic Development, "About Us," http://www.insightcced.org/ (accessed June 10, 2010).

8. Participant comment, Catholic Charities USA 21st Century Solutions to Poverty Forum.

9. "Statewide Anti-poverty Initiatives," http://www.spotlightonpoverty.org/ (accessed June 10, 2010).

10. Dedication of the Hubert H. Humphrey Building, November 1, 1977, Congressional Record 123 (November 4, 1977), 37287, http://list.uvm.edu/.

Chapter 7: Acting Anew

1. Karen de Sá, "Silicon Valley agencies unite to cut poverty by 2020," *Mercury News*, April 20, 2009, http://www.stepupsv.com/ (accessed June 15, 2010).

2. "What Is Time Banking All About?" http://www.timebanks.org/how-it-works.htm.

3. http://www.detroitagriculture.org/GRP.

4. http://www.dinnergarden.org/index.html.

5. http://www.ccsinashville.org/.

6. U.S. Department of Health and Human Services, *Oral Health in*

America: A Report of the Surgeon General—Executive Summary (Rockville, MD: U.S. Department of Health and Human Services, National Institute of Dental and Craniofacial Research, National Institutes of Health, 2000), http://www2.nidcr.nih.gov/.

7. U.S. Census Bureau, "Projections of the Population by Selected Age Groups and Sex for the United States: 2010 to 2050," http://www.census.gov/.

8. AARP Public Policy Institute, "Developing Appropriate Rental Housing for Low-Income Older Persons: A Survey of Section 202 and LIHTC Property Managers," 2006.

9. Ibid.

Chapter 8: To Think and Act Anew

1. The Catholic Worker Movement, www.catholicworker.org/ (accessed June 10, 2010).

Appendix A
Centennial Recognition Program Award Winners of Catholic Charities USA

During this year of regional leadership summits, Catholic Charities USA has recognized local Catholic Charities agencies for programs that are effective in reducing poverty in America. These programs demonstrate strong work and focused efforts that can inspire others.

Project H.O.P.E.
Catholic Charities Community Services, Phoenix, AZ

Project H.O.P.E. (Help Out of Poverty forEver) assists people in generational poverty live a life of security, stability, and satisfaction. The program offers a continuum of services to help people investigate their own lives, develop skills, and obtain social capital, resulting in a better future.

The Diocesan Immigration Support Network
Catholic Charities of Sacramento, Inc., CA

This program provides leadership training and ongoing support to parish leaders appointed by their pastor. These leaders mobilize their parish community in support of the advocacy efforts of the U.S. bishops to bring about comprehensive immigration reform; conduct listening campaigns in their parishes to surface parishioners' concerns related to immigration; build relationships with local elected or community officials, such as city and county government, business leaders, and law enforcement; and organize their parish community to advocate for changes in structures to keep people out of poverty.

Family to Family Partnership
Catholic Charities of the East Bay, Oakland, CA

The Family to Family Partnership is a family-strengthening program that helps families improve the quality of their lives by empowering them toward self-sufficiency. The program, which currently includes thirteen churches and sixteen parish teams, is built on the belief that personal connections between parishes and clients play a critical role in helping families become economically self-sufficient.

The Thomas Merton Campus
Catholic Charities of Fairfield County, CT

The Thomas Merton Campus is located in the heart of the poorest area (the Hollow) in Bridgeport, the largest and poorest city in Connecticut. The campus addresses all five issue areas of Catholic Charities USA's Campaign to Reduce Poverty in America—providing medical services, a soup kitchen, a community garden with local churches of all denominations, housing for families, and a family center that provides training and educational assistance. The Thomas Merton Center is a fully contained, holistic approach to fighting the poverty battle and creating a ladder of human dignity.

Fortitude Housing
Catholic Charities of the Archdiocese of Washington, DC

The Fortitude Housing initiative strengthens the lives of over one hundred formerly homeless residents of the District of Columbia placed in permanent supportive housing through intensive case management services. Fortitude Housing recognizes the fundamental importance of housing to provide the incentive, stability, and strength for people to escape the cycle of chronic homelessness. The impact Fortitude Housing has on reducing material poverty is unquestionable, but it also celebrates the good news proclaimed to the poor by providing help and creating hope and new beginnings for the chronically homeless.

Pathways to Economic Stability
Catholic Charities of Idaho

Pathways to Economic Stability provides a range of services to improve a family's economic position and increase stability, including resume/interview workshops, computer training, and financial education. The program helps individuals gain skills and confidence to build assets and break out of the cycle of poverty. In addition to financial training, the program offers supportive services such as counseling, parenting education, and citizenship/immigration guidance.

St. Leo Campus
Catholic Charities of the Archdiocese of Chicago, IL

The St. Leo Campus is comprised of four different programs designed to improve the community's capacity to serve its veterans through stable housing, job training, addiction support, and counseling. All of Catholic Charities Veterans Initiatives are designed to help formerly homeless veterans achieve self-sufficiency and prevent homelessness by offering employment services and through providing affordable housing for senior veterans.

Provide Help Create Hope
Catholic Charities of Louisville, KY

This program helps local parishes respond more effectively and efficiently to those in need, whether situational or chronic, and provides case management and assistance directly to families and individuals, helping them re-establish stability and hope. While not neglecting those who have been in chronic need, a particular focus of the project is those newly affected by current economic conditions, people in "situational" and not "chronic" crisis. Provide Help Create Hope serves as a lead partner with the archdiocese, its parishes, and other community resources, to bring the existing foundation and resources of Catholic Charities to shape and lead an effective response and reduce the instances of future crises.

Christopher Place Employment Academy
Catholic Charities of the Archdiocese of Baltimore, MD

Christopher Place Employment Academy (CPEA) is an intensive eighteen-month residential program that provides education and training as well as emotional, spiritual, and addiction recovery support to formerly homeless men. The academy invites participants to engage in a process of change that moves them from homelessness to permanent stable living, trains them to obtain employment, and empowers them to live a life free of drugs and alcohol. The facility eliminates the challenges faced by men as they merely survive and allows them to focus on mastering necessary life-skills, enabling the men to achieve independent freedom. Graduates of CPEA re-enter their communities as enlightened, self-sufficient, caring, and spiritually whole men.

The Caritas Center's Continuum of Care
Catholic Charities of Kansas City – St. Joseph, MO

This family center offers a continuum of comprehensive programs and strong advocacy for all clients. The mission and programs focus on reducing poverty through an innovative, dual strategy. The dual approach addresses the wide-ranging needs of clients in the moment and geography of their need, while further empowering and strengthening grassroots social service agencies across the region to successfully combat the formidable strains of poverty.

St. Patrick Center
Catholic Charities, Archdiocese of St. Louis, MO

Founded in 1983, this agency has served over 132,000 homeless and impoverished people since its inception and now provides comprehensive, holistic services for about 9,000 people each year. The center's 28 programs are designed to take extremely disadvantaged individuals from mere subsistence to lifelong self-sufficiency. The center focuses on the three basic areas that contribute to ongoing homelessness and poverty—housing, employment, and mental health.

Recipe for Success
New Hampshire Catholic Charities, NH

Recipe for Success is a four-part program of the New Hampshire Food Bank, run by New Hampshire Catholic Charities, that combines job training, nutrition education, fresh food rescue, and a community garden to help serve people in our community who are at risk of hunger. A certified affiliate of Feeding America, the New Hampshire Food Bank is the only food warehouse distribution center in the state. Last year, close to six million pounds of donated and surplus food was distributed to more than four hundred pantries, soup kitchens, shelters, day-care centers, senior-citizen homes, and substance abuse treatment centers across the state.

St. Bridget's HIV/AIDS Support Network
Catholic Charities of the Archdiocese of Newark, NJ

The St. Bridget's HIV/AIDS Support Network enables HIV-positive persons to maintain access to the continuum of HIV services through the incorporation of integral service components including case management, substance abuse services, and nutritionally balanced meals within emergency and transitional housing settings. The HIV/AIDS Support Network, which started out to meet the need of homeless individuals with HIV/AIDS for a place to go during the day, has become an established multiservice community program.

Wheels for Work
Catholic Charities of the Diocese of Albany, NY

Launched in 2001, Wheels for Work invites individuals and families residing in the local communities of upstate New York to donate their used cars to Catholic Charities. In turn, these vehicles are mechanically serviced and given to individuals and families whose household incomes fall within 200 percent of the federal poverty guidelines. While the lack of car ownership can contribute to individuals staying in lower-paying jobs and/or not securing better paying positions, Catholic Charities has found that other underlying factors may keep a number of families entrenched in poverty, namely lack of education, low skill sets, inadequate housing, and medical and child-care issues. The Wheels for Work caseworkers provide case management to identify these interfering variables and work with the applicants to find their way through these barriers.

Closing the Gap in Student Performance
Catholic Charities of Buffalo, NY

Closing the Gap in Student Performance (CTG) is a school-based collaboration currently embedded in eight of the lowest performing pre-kindergarten through eighth grade, Buffalo Public Schools, serving over four thousand students. CTG integrates health, human, and social services to enhance conditions for learning in partnership with leaders in the school and the district. CTG promotes resiliency, helps students to succeed academically and socially, and provides necessary family support, allowing teachers to teach and administrators to lead and plan.

Catholic Charities Housing Transitions
Catholic Charities, Portland, OR

Catholic Charities Housing Transitions provides permanent housing to homeless and chronically homeless women in the Portland area. The program serves women facing multiple barriers to housing and provides varying amounts of financial support as they acquire enough income to maintain housing on their own.

Elizabeth's Homes
Catholic Charities of East Tennessee, TN

Through Elizabeth's Homes homeless families are able to obtain housing self-sufficiency, increase skills and/or income, and achieve greater self-determination. During the two-year program, supportive relationships are fostered among the clients who are housed in scattered sites. Three case workers are responsible for twenty-six families in three geographic areas within Eastern Tennessee, the majority of which serve rural communities. This program is built to reduce poverty one family at a time through a case management and housing process that makes use of wrap-around services in order to foster client self-determination. Case management promotes career enhancement and job placement, and the educational process includes everything from basic homemaking skills to household budgeting.

Adoption Support and Preservation Program
Catholic Charities of Tennessee, Inc., TN

The Adoption Support and Preservation Program provides in-home therapeutic services, support groups, parent training, and community advocacy to families who have adopted children from the State of Tennessee's foster care system. The therapy is designed to improve family relationships and resolution of past trauma and losses that may impede the child's ability to function successfully. Research continues to show the statistical correlation between foster care and poverty. Children aging out of the foster care system are among the most vulnerable population in the nation. As the children in the adoptive families served by the Adoption Support and Preservation Program have a more stable adolescence, they enter adulthood more prepared for independence.

The HOMES Program
Catholic Charities of Fort Worth, TX

The HOMES program works with chronic homeless individuals and families to find a permanent end to each person's homelessness. The program works with individuals through every step of the process, beginning with initial engagement on the street or in shelters. Through every interaction with the program's previously homeless individuals, the program staff use a strengths-based, client-centered approach.

Phoenix Housing Network
Catholic Charities of Western Washington, WA

Phoenix Housing Network provides a broad continuum of services to homeless families with children under the age of eighteen and to households at risk of becoming homeless. Their programs encourage change toward self-sufficiency by having participants develop a Family Transition Plan based on their unique family needs and strengths. On-going case management ensures participants progress with their plans.

Tepeyac Haven
Catholic Charities of Spokane, WA

Tepeyac Haven is a 45-unit affordable housing complex that serves migrant farm laborers. The program helps workers settle into housing, become stable in the community, and begin to build assets.

Financial Health Counseling
Catholic Charities of the Diocese of Green Bay, WI

This budget and debt counseling services program is rooted in the belief that a strong family and community is the ultimate goal. To strengthen financial well-being, the program looks at housing, individual development accounts, business partnerships, community awareness, diversity circles, and predatory lending practices.

For more information on these and other programs to reduce poverty visit the recognition program website at www.catholiccharitiesusa.org.

Appendix B
Ideas from Catholic Charities USA Regional Summits

During the regional summits that were held around the country in 2009 and 2010, participants held small-group roundtable discussions to pool their collective experiences and develop a short list of ideas to explore in the campaign to reduce poverty in America. Some of their ideas, which were quickly jotted down during the meetings, are listed below and are a good start to "thinking anew." Developing them into real programs will enable us to also "act anew."

1. Initiate long-term programs that help people become self-sufficient.
2. Promote financial education and asset-building.
3. Improve marketing of the Earned Income Tax Credit (EITC), the Volunteer Income Tax Assistance (VITA), and earned benefits.
4. Make food stamp application services available at all food pantries.
5. Systematize state assistance programs to have online applications available.
6. Coordinate both governmental and non-governmental outreach programs to prevent duplication of services and network across issues.
7. Implement a living wage.
8. Establish outreach programs on the streets to raise awareness of victims of poverty.
9. Campaign explicitly for the well-being of people from a moral standpoint, not a political agenda.
10. Focus on educating and communicating with clients in a plain and understandable manner.
11. Promote housing to be safe and affordable, including access to services that cater to all ages and social conditions.

12. Design social programs with the flexibility to be tailored for each individual's needs in order to result in a positive life change.
13. Renew and update the Older Americans Act.
14. Increase the nutritional content of school lunches and address the summer-time gap by possibly having churches supply meals.
15. Offer and encourage leadership development as part of social programs for greater consumer engagement: "Nothing about us without us."
16. Begin pilot projects small and grow them with the help of funding from the business community/strategic partnerships as the project proves successful.
17. Draw on the real-life experiences of clients as an instrument of political advocacy.
18. Focus on permanent change through holistic programs that are creative and have government and community support.
19. Use a three-prong approach to people's needs: "Rescue, Support and Development."
20. Balance reactive and proactive programs.
21. Make funding for housing and caring for the disadvantaged a top priority.
22. Facilitate early intervention to keep children in school.
23. Make programs adaptable so as to meet the needs of both urban and suburban clients.
24. Enrich programs that work and pattern others after them.
25. Encourage programs that center on self-sufficiency for an overall more successful outcome.
26. Implement needs assessment and client satisfaction tools/ surveys.
27. Obtain supplies as donations from the corporate sector.
28. Never terminate your client.
29. Create a partnership with clients.
30. Foster community involvement.
31. Promote an understanding of the culture of poverty.
32. Form an alliance with IRS programs, e.g., VITA.

33. Make health care available to all.
34. Lead a campaign of immigration reform.
35. Dioceses and agencies, from the top down, need to work together in a comprehensive and holistic manner, from funding through actualization.
36. Award Catholic Charities' business service contracts (e.g., food services and cleaning services) to local small businesses that hire unemployed workers through our social programs.
37. Train law enforcement to understand mental illness, which in turn reduces arrests and therefore the number of inmates.
38. Use Haven for Hope's paradigm of collaboration as a model for other social programs.
39. Provide education for all aspects of living, i.e., parenting, financial, etc.
40. Improve information sharing to promote best practices.
41. Enhance capacity assessment to ensure adequate space for programs.
42. Endorse corporate social responsibility.
43. Enlist multi-directional education within and outside of the client base.
44. Renew efforts to respond to the needs of those experiencing hardship.
45. Require corporate institutions to provide both vocational and public training.
46. Publicize the consequences of early interruption of education.
47. Find new models for breaking the cycle of poverty/homelessness by appealing to both the child and the parents.
48. Provide education for parents on parenting.
49. Develop channels of communication between agencies for collaboration.
50. Require private and public sectors to support community institutions.
51. Listen to the needs of the people through outreach in their own communities.
52. Enhance the quality of job training, improve the availability of better jobs, and institute a living wage.
53. Cultivate an open dialogue among governmental, non-profit,

and faith-based organizations to facilitate economic development.

54. Promote an honest dialogue that can advance common goals shared by organizations through cooperation and working together.

55. Petition lawmakers to promote a better understanding regarding the needs of those who benefit from government-funded charities.

56. Address the need for cross-institutional communication and planning.

57. Create models of communication that all agencies can use as a guide.

58. Highlight the positive effects of successful collaborations in order to promote working together.

59. Highlight the ways in which successful companies benefit from collaboration.

60. Launch a greater effort for communicating the need for parish involvement with social justice and service.

61. Child abuse prevention is continuous work and needs to be addressed with a multifaceted approach.

62. Solicit ideas for inventive ways for Catholic Charities to increase fundraising.

63. Approach problem solving with a spiritual purpose.

64. Create more opportunities for parents to interact with their child's educators.

65. Facilitate resiliency and faith training.

66. Encourage parents to volunteer in their child's school.

67. Create client-run support groups and talking circles.

68. Re-think social service models and implement successful methods used in non-governmental organizations.

69. Reinforce optional systems and facilitate multiple systems communication for best possible outcomes.

70. Create entry points into the social system.

71. Advocate for legislation that is not onerous, but that facilitates progress in people's efforts to leave poverty behind.

72. Change the way we deliver services to make them more effective.

73. Extend programs that are working and phase out those that aren't.
74. Enlist others in small and large ways to bring awareness to the issue, e.g., your children, politicians, celebrities.
75. Design functional programs that bring optimal results.
76. Bring "Transition to Community" ideas into the college classroom.
77. Take opportunities in childhood education to train children in all aspects of living a productive and happy life.
78. Campaign for changes in the tax code to fairly distribute resources.
79. Establish funding programs for educating those in need with postponed repayment at a reasonable and fair rate.
80. Promote the betterment of the community through the involvement of each individual within it.
81. Establish intra-community relationships for the advancement of all.
82. Reference the book *Paradigm Found: Leading and Managing for Positive Change,* by Anne Firth Murray, as a template for building outstanding programs.
83. Enlist the locals to decide what steps should be taken to eliminate poverty in their community.
84. Seize this opportunity to talk about poverty as the face of the poor has changed.
85. Help people to break the cycle of poverty, not only through higher education, but through esteem-building as well, especially for those who cannot further their formal education.
86. Provide opportunities for people to change their lives and break the patterns of their forerunners by making deep human connections within their family and with other community members.
87. Establish programs that enable schools and families to work together to raise the young.
88. Create a system of open scholarships for needy students that require them to give back service in exchange for higher education.
89. Institute social programs that need minimal start-up capital

and can be perpetuated through the service of those who were helped.

90. Modify the health-care system to address the needs of children who are not established in a stable location.

91. Promote a better world by enlisting the help of community members and leading by example.

92. Enact an earned income tax credit for volunteerism.

93. Increase a child's ability to be successful by establishing a strong beginning through child assistance programs.

94. Update Federal Poverty Guidelines to reflect the current situation so more people can be eligible for getting more assistance.

95. Use Sarah's Oasis in St. Paul, Minnesota, as a prototype for women's shelters.

96. Establish the credibility of the "web of poverty" in the media as an opportunity to educate the public on the many aspects of social behavior that promote poverty.

97. Leverage the current economic situation to take action against the systemic roots of poverty.

98. Become committed to eliminating poverty and homelessness in the future by taking action to address the complexity of the problem today.

99. The key to solving the problem of homelessness is the need to address the problems of each individual situation with a multifaceted approach.

100. It's a lot harder to get someone out of poverty than it is to address the problem before it happens.

101. We have to look at the social determinants of poverty for women.

102. Abandon the temptation to blame, and eliminate guilt, alienation, and distrust.

103. Reach out to start-up companies and get them to assure the participation of employees in volunteering for social causes.

104. Get involved with developers in your community to provide housing for the homeless.

105. Encourage parents to be involved in the community and to take on leadership responsibilities to help them overcome the stagnation of poverty.

106. Entrepreneurial education can promote competence and confidence, especially for those who have lost jobs.
107. There is immense power in opportunities for students to engage with the poor to promote community-based learning.
108. Build a community by connecting different social outreach programs to foster a larger network of promoting personal relationships.
109. Family-to-family volunteerism consolidates resources and has proven to be transformative for those who participate, fostering excitement, energy, and celebration.
110. Create a partnership with local grocery stores via a food voucher program that becomes a gateway into getting clients into other programs.
111. We have to enlist the poor themselves as well as the leaders of low-income communities to help create social programs to benefit all.
112. We need to go beyond micro-lending because of the difference between necessity entrepreneurs and opportunity entrepreneurs.
113. Engage your clients in the political process when possible, especially in voting.
114. Endorse the seven focus areas of the Poverty Reduction Symposium: child care, economics, food, health, housing, neighborhood development, and workforce development.
115. Harness the power of social media to inspire conversation into action.
116. We must embrace politics.
117. See the solution to poverty in the words of the people who are impoverished.
118. Create products that foster financial education.
119. Foster collaboration between all service groups within a community to streamline services and better use funding.
120. Policies and practices must be created by legislators, service organizations, *and* those being served.
121. Integrate services within an organization as well as with other community services.
122. Engage young people in the movement to eliminate poverty by

making it a viable career option starting with post-secondary education.

123. Design health-care services to address deep healing by offering comprehensive and diverse services including complementary and alternative medicine.

124. Services available should include programs as diverse as traditional housing, job training, and art therapy.

125. Build better communities by focusing on the needs of each individual community so that the health of the people, environment, and economy are addressed.

126. Include a network of dentists in health services for the poor.

127. Provide quality nursing home benefits for those without medical coverage.

128. Work with clients with the intention to change their lives for the better in a permanent manner.

129. Policy changes need to consider all resources available in this day and age, including new technologies, for the most effective outcomes.

130. Impose a moratorium on foreclosures as there is no benefit to the communities or banks in having abandoned houses.

131. Concentrate efforts in job training to lead to employment that will provide adequate income.

132. Stop poverty before it starts by bolstering childhood education.

133. A community must have an economy of basic services, such as banks and grocery stores, before the issue of poverty can be addressed.

134. Public and private transportation needs to be adequate and affordable to enable those who are able to work to get to work.

135. Provide job specific training to create a strong workforce.

136. Offer assistance in resume writing, job search, interview skills, etc. to provide better access to the local job market.

137. Keep tax incentives in place even during times of tax reform.

138. Extend social service resources and access to housing to students.

139. Inspire the community to become involved with the social issues that affect their neighborhood.

140. Offer affordable child care and easy access to quality elementary schools.
141. Establish accessible parent education opportunities.
142. Create peer mentoring programs.
143. Provide counseling and assistance with all aspects of searching for a job as well as continuing education.
144. Rebuild neighborhoods by establishing an infrastructure of social services that is easily accessible.
145. Address regional economic development in a manner that results in the elimination of poverty in all communities.
146. Construct a community through the collaborative efforts and strategic planning by all who live within it.
147. Address the needs of the individual members of the family with an age-appropriate approach for the best possible effect on the family as a whole.

Suggested Resources

In Print

Blond, Phillip. "The Civic State—ResPublica," in ResPublica, Changing the Terms of Debate. *ResPublica* (3 October 2009), http://www.respublica.org.uk/articles/civic-state.

Blond, Phillip. *Red Tory: How the Left and Right Have Broken Britain and How We Can Fix It.* New York: Faber and Faber, 2010.

Burd-Sharps, Sarah, Kristen Lewis, and Eduardo Borges Martins, eds. *The Measure of America: American Human Development Report 2008-2009.* New York: SSRC/Columbia University Press, 2008.

Catholic Charities USA. *The Home Is the Foundation*, 2008.

Catholic Charities USA. *Poverty and Racism: Overlapping Threats to the Common Good*, 2007.

Catholic Charities USA. *Poverty in America: A Threat to the Common Good*, 2006.

Clark, C. and Sr. Helen Alford, O.P. *Rich and Poor: Rebalancing the Economy.* London: Catholic Truth Society, 2010.

Danforth, Senator Dan, *Faith and Politics: How the "Moral Values" Debate Divides America and How to Move Forward Together.* New York: Penguin Books, 2006.

DeVol, Philip E., Ruby K. Payne, and Terie Dreussi Smith. *Bridges out of Poverty: Strategies for Professionals and Communities: Workbook.* Highlands, TX: aha!Process, 2006.

Dionne, E. J. *Souled Out: Reclaiming Politics after the Religious Right.* Princeton: Princeton University Press, 2008.

Edelman, Peter, Harry Holzer, and Paul Offner. *Reconnecting Disadvantaged Young Men.* Washington, DC: Urban Institute Press, 2006.

Ehlige, Bill and Ruby Payne. *What Every Church Member Should Know about Poverty*. Highlands, TX: aha! Process, Inc., 2005.

Goldsmith, Stephen. *The Power of Social Innovation: How Civic Entrepreneurs Ignite Community Networks for Good*. San Francisco: Jossey-Bass, 2010.

_____. *Putting Faith in Neighborhoods: Making Cities Work through Grassroots Citizenship*. Noblesville, IN: Hudson Institute, 2002.

Grossman, Allen, William Foster, and Catherine Ross. "Youth Villages," *Harvard Business Review* (6 November 2008), http://hbr.org/product/youth-villages/an/309007-PDF-ENG.

Hehir, Bryan J., ed. *Catholic Charities USA: 100 Years at the Intersection of Charity and Justice*. Collegeville, MN: Liturgical Press, 2010.

"How Much Is Enough in Your County? The 2008 California Family Economic Self–Sufficiency Standard," May 2008, http://www.insightcced.org/uploads/cfes/sss-exec-summ-final-050908.pdf.

Iceland, John. *Poverty in America*. Berkeley: University of California Press, 2006.

Longman, Phillip and Ray Boshara. *The Next Progressive Era: A Blueprint for Broad Prosperity*. Washington, DC: New America Foundation, 2009.

Myers-Lipton, Scott J., and Charles Lemert. *Social Solutions to Poverty: America's Struggle to Build a Just Society*. Illustrated edition. Boulder, CO: Paradigm, 2007.

Opportunity NYC Report, March 2010, http://www.mdrc.org/publications/549/full.pdf.

President's Advisory Council on Faith-Based and Neighborhood Partnerships. *A New Era of Partnerships: Report of Recommendations to the President*, 2010.

Rank, Mark Robert. *One Nation, Underprivileged*. New York: Oxford University Press, 2005.

Sachs, Jeffrey. *The End of Poverty: Economic Possibilities for Our Time*. New York: Penguin Books, 2005.

Shipler, David K. *The Working Poor: Invisible in America*. New York: Vintage Books, 2005.

Sperling, Gene. *The Pro-Growth Progressive: An Economic Strategy for Shared Prosperity*. New York: Simon and Schuster, 2005.

Step Up Silicon Valley Action Plan, April 2009, http://www.catholiccharitiesscc.org/stepupsv/images/StepUpSiliconValley_ActionPlanReport.pdf.

U.S. Conference of Catholic Bishops. *Economic Justice for All, Pastoral Letter on Catholic Social Teaching and the U.S. Economy*. Washington, DC: USCCB, 1986.

Yunus, Muhammad. *Building Social Business: The New Kind of Capitalism That Serves Humanity's Most Pressing Needs*. New York: PublicAffairs Books, 2010.

Yunus, Mohammed with Karl Weber. *Creating a World without Poverty: How Social Business Can Transform Our Lives*. New York: PublicAffairs Books, 2009.

On the Internet

Annie E. Casey Foundation—www.aecf.org.

Brookings Institution—www.Brookings.org.

Catholic Campaign for Human Development—www.usccb.org/cchd.

Catholic Charities USA—www.catholiccharitiesusa.org.

Center for Responsible Lending—www.responsiblelending.org.

CFED—www.CFED.org.

Children's Defense Fund—www.childrensdefense.org.

Economic Policy Institute—www.EPI.org.

The Heritage Foundation—www.heritage.org.

Kids Count—www.kidscount.org.

Measure of America—www.measureofamerica.org.

The National Center for Children in Poverty (NCCP)—www.NCCP.org.

New America Foundation—www.NewAmerica.net.

Northwest Area Foundation—www.nwaf.org.

Office of Faith-based and Neighborhood Partnerships:—http://www.whitehouse.gov/administration/eop/ofbnp.

The Pew Forum on Religion and Public Life—www.pewforum.org.

Spotlight on Poverty—www.spotlightonpoverty.org/.

U.S. Census Bureau—www.Census.gov.

About the Author

In February 2005, Rev. Larry Snyder took the helm of Catholic Charities USA (CCUSA)—the national office of more than 1,700 local Catholic Charities agencies and institutions nationwide that provide help and create hope for more than nine million people a year, regardless of their religious, social, or economic backgrounds.

Just six months after his arrival at CCUSA, Father Snyder led the network's largest disaster recovery efforts in its history in response to Hurricanes Katrina and Rita, in which more than 110 Catholic Charities in the Gulf Coast and beyond provided immediate and long-term aid to over one million victims of the hurricanes.

Today, Father Snyder oversees Catholic Charities USA's work to reduce poverty in America. This multi-year, multi-faceted initiative aims to cut poverty in half by 2020, urging Congress and the administration to give a much higher priority to the needs of the poor in budget and policy decisions.

In February, President Barack Obama appointed Father Snyder to the newly created President's Council of Faith-based and Neighborhood Partnerships. The council will work with the Office of Faith-based and Neighborhood Partnerships to advise the president and administration on how government and nonprofits can better work together. On this council, Father Snyder will work with other religious and community leaders of diverse political, religious, and community backgrounds from across the country.